W0246815

Philosophy and India

Philosophy and India

Ancestors, Outsiders, and Predecessors

A. Raghuramaraju

OXFORD
UNIVERSITY PRESS

OXFORD
UNIVERSITY PRESS

Oxford University Press is a department of the University of Oxford.
It furthers the University's objective of excellence in research, scholarship,
and education by publishing worldwide. Oxford is a registered trademark of
Oxford University Press in the UK and in certain other countries

Published in India by
Oxford University Press
YMCA Library Building, 1 Jai Singh Road, New Delhi 110 001, India

© Oxford University Press 2013

The moral rights of the author have been asserted

First Edition published in 2013

All rights reserved. No part of this publication may be reproduced, stored in
a retrieval system, or transmitted, in any form or by any means, without the
prior permission in writing of Oxford University Press, or as expressly permitted
by law, by licence, or under terms agreed with the appropriate reprographics
rights organization. Enquiries concerning reproduction outside the scope of the
above should be sent to the Rights Department, Oxford University Press, at the
address above

You must not circulate this book in any other form
and you must impose this same condition on any acquirer

ISBN-13: 978-0-19-809223-0
ISBN-10: 0-19-809223-7

Typeset in Fournier MT Std 11.5/14
by Alphæta Solutions, Puducherry, India 605 009
Printed in India by Artxel, Noida 201 301

To
Ashis Nandy and Uma Nandy
with affection

Alas, a jeweler has come into the flower garden

He wants to appraise the truth of a lotus by rubbing it against his touchstone

(Rural poet quoted by Rabindranath Tagore in his *Pathway to Mukti*)

CONTENTS

ACKNOWLEDGEMENTS

The first chapter, 'Advaita to Kant', was previously published with the title 'Krishna Chandra Bhattacharyya on the Unknowability of Self in Kant: Problematizing the Programme of Indian Remedies to Western Problems', in *Reason, Morality and Beauty: Essays on the Philosophy of Immanuel Kant*, edited by Bindu Puri and Heiko Sievers, New Delhi: Oxford University Press, 2007. The second chapter, 'Gandhi to Western Moral Philosophy', was published with the title 'Forgotten Moral Exemplars of the West: A Critique of Akeel Bilgrami's Projection of Gandhi', in *Grounding Morality: Freedom, Knowledge and the Plurality of Cultures*, edited by Jyotirmaya Sharma and A. Raghuramaraju, New Delhi: Routledge, 2010. I thank Routledge for giving the permission to reprint it here.

Previous versions of some chapters were presented at seminars at Panjab University, Chandigarh; Pondicherry University, Puducherry; Max Mueller Bhavan, New Delhi and Chennai; Jadavpur University, Kolkata; Smith College, Northampton; Sahitya Akademi, New Delhi; University of Rajasthan, Jaipur; Indian Institute of Advanced Study, Shimla; University of Delhi; Manipal University; Jawaharlal Nehru University, New Delhi; North-Eastern Hill University, Shillong; Andhra University, Vishakhapatnam; and the Indian Council of Philosophical Research, New Delhi. I thank the following for their invitations to present the papers—Mrinal Miri, Sujata Miri, Ashok Vohra, Bindu Puri, V. Sanil, Alok Bhalla, Jay L. Garfield, Nalini Bhushan, Sharad Deshpande, V. T. Sebastian, Oinam Bhagat, R. P. Singh, P. K. Dutta, Sukumar, Vanlaghank, Shail Mayaram, Godavarish Misra, and Sujata and Sanjay Kumar.

I thank the following for their critical comments on these papers at various stages in their development—Ashis Nandy, Akeel Bilgrami, Mrinal Miri, Gopal Guru, S. Shaji, Vakulabharanam Rajagopal, Sudhir Chandra, Gitanjali Sri, Venkat Rao, Vadrevu China Veerabhadrudu, and Purushottam Aggarwal. Sundar Sarukkai and Dhanwanti Nayak provided me much-needed motivation when I was running out of wits. Sundar's invitation to lecture both at National Institute of Advanced Studies, Bengaluru, and Manipal University, and his reassurance has given me confidence and energy to finish this work. I am extremely thankful to both of them. I am indebted to Aparna Davare for thoroughly reading through the manuscript and giving critical insights, which helped me revise it.

Thom Brook in his review of my book *Debates in Indian Philosophy* (Raghuramaraju 2006) pointed out that the book's 'focus is entirely on Indian philosophers who are Hindu'. He quite rightly says—'This gives the misleading impression that Hindu philosophers are the only figures of importance in contemporary Indian debates...I was very surprised to find no mention at all of B. R. Ambedkar, a Buddhist convert...' This comment made me rethink but I proceeded slowly on this and seriously started thinking about Ambedkar. There is a small but substantial reference to him in my later book *Enduring Colonialism: Classical Presences and Modern Absences in Indian Philosophy* (2009); a larger place in the next one titled *Modernity in Indian Social Theory* (2011); and more in this book where I bring him more directly than I was capable of earlier. I thank Thom Brook for this perceptive observation which continues to be productive in my philosophical activity. I am also thankful to two anonymous reviewers of Oxford University Press who have made some significant critical remarks which made me revise the book.

Laxminaraya Kadekar and Jyotirmaya Sharma's wise counseling soothed my pain and anger and calmed me down, enabling me to complete this work. For this I am immensely thankful to both of them. Gurava Reddy provided our children with much-needed direction which gave me stability. I am extremely thankful to Rajeswari Miskha Sinha for her generosity in making substantial corrections to the manuscript. Discussions with her gave me clarity and considerably decreased the underlying ambiguities which otherwise would have obscured ideas in the text. I am extremely thankful to R. V. Harnoor for a thorough copy-editing of the text. I fondly remember my neighbours C. Krishna Mohan Rao, Vijaya Mohan, C. Kavita, Siva Raju, and Krishnama Raju, and thank them for their help. A special thanks to Bharat Kumar, D. Balaganapathi, Anand B. Sagar, D. Balasubramanyam, Anjaiah, Rajasekaram, Maha Lakshmi, and Gayathri Durga for sustaining my interest in this project. Finally, my family has disciplined and helped bring about some order in my life which is so necessary to handle texts. I fondly remember my parents, Seetha Rama Raju and Kannemma, wife, Jyothy, and children, Vatsalya and Venu.

This book is affectionately dedicated to Ashis Nandy and Uma. Uma*ji* has always been affectionate towards me and my family. *Dada* took interest in my work, regularly enquired about what I was doing, and encouraged me with appropriate advice. I fondly remember their love and affection.

INTRODUCTION

Rabindranath Tagore, a poet, was invited to deliver the inaugural Presidential address at the Indian Philosophical Congress. Sarvepalli Radhakrishnan, an Indian philosopher, internationally recognized for his work on the subject, was chosen as the President of India, the country's highest office. The poet's humble, wise, and fascinating address to the Congress has long been forgotten, and despite the global acclaim of Radhakrishnan, philosophy in India subsequently did not make a mark.

However, it is 'in philosophy, if anywhere', claims Krishna Chandra Bhattacharyya,

> that the task of discovering the soul of India is imperative for modern India; the task of achieving, if possible, the continuity of his old self with his present day self, of realising what is nowadays called the Mission of India, if it has any. Genius can unveil the soul of India in art but it is through philosophy that we can methodically attempt to discover it. (1984: 386–7)

So, philosophy is the terrain that can systematically explicate the soul of India. It is philosophy that can accomplish the mission that Bhattacharyya evokes of modern India. In Bhattacharyya's reckoning, philosophy is not just another subject. It is *the* central mode of knowledge that can carry on its shoulders the tasks of civilization.

Notwithstanding its true capacity and assigned centrality, philosophy in modern India has not lived up to fulfilling this task. Taking cognizance of this history, this book embarks on the

project of critically assessing the contributions of some of the serious
academic philosophers of India. The book is divided into three parts.
Chapters 1 and 2 discuss the project of offering Indian solutions for
Western problems. The first chapter analyses Krishna Chandra
Bhattacharyya's offer of Advaita as a solution to the Kantian problem of the unknowability of the self. Unlike Gandhi, who sought
for internal resources to deal with the problem of India and the
West, Bhattacharyya traverses a path more akin to that of Bankim,
Vivekananda, and Aurobindo. Without first seeking the solutions for
Kant within the West, he offers solutions from India, or, more specifically, from Advaita. Similarly, Akeel Bilgrami, while discussing
an entirely different problem, traverses the same path where he too
without first seeking exemplars from the West, such as Socrates or
Christ, offers Gandhi's views of exemplar as a way out for solving
the problems surrounding Western moral philosophy. In this context,
I point out how their projects present an inverted version of colonial thematic. The colonial thematic, for instance, constructs India
as a reservoir of problems and the West as a reservoir of solutions
to those problems. The larger theoretical problem in these versions,
the original colonial version and its inversion in Bhattacharyya and
Bilgrami, persists in the underlying assumptions both make about the
essentiality of East and West. I suggest an alternative binary, that lies
between pre-modern and modern, which, being more inclusive and
pluralistic, is closer to Gandhi than the East–West binary described
earlier. The third chapter critiques the project of B. K. Matilal, who
invests the epic Mahabharata with the task of incorporating ethics for
Indian philosophy. This is problematic—while both Bhattacharyya
and Bilgrami point out the limitations in Western philosophy and
morality, Matilal strives to fill a lacuna in Indian philosophy, namely,
that it does not include an ethical dimension. This chapter shows
how the purview of 'epic' is greater than 'ethics' and Matilal's offer
falls short of a good bargain. One of the major surplus aspects of the
epic is its capacity for regional access. In this context, the chapter
discusses how the Mahabharata has, with the advent of modernity,
entered the vernacular literatures, in disguise.

The second part has two chapters. The first chapter discusses the philosophical assumptions of the *Samvāda* project undertaken by Daya Krishna and others. It lays bare the temporal imbalance underlying this project, that is, how this project tried to bring modern Western philosophy into dialogue with traditional Indian philosophy. The chapter argues that this imbalance is responsible for the failure of their project. The project failed because it recalled those classical texts that were sent on sabbatical with the arrival of modernity, and colonialism, in India. These texts, which largely inhabit a terrain comprising inequalities and hierarchies, are, with the entrance of egalitarian systems, not necessarily destroyed, but placed on sabbatical. Recalling these texts is bound to be counter-productive. The second chapter critically evaluates K. Satchidananda Murty's assessment of the state of philosophy in Indian universities. Although Murty's philosophical canvas is very wide, in his assessment of the state of philosophy in India, he fails to take into consideration the contributions from the *sandhi* period—the late nineteenth and early twentieth centuries. This part of the book shows how both Daya Krishna and Satchidananda Murty are largely preoccupied with ancestors and outsiders and have grossly neglected their immediate predecessors. These predecessors, consisting of Vivekananda, Aurobindo, Gandhi, and others, seriously negotiated, with varying degrees of success, both ancestors and outsiders. This attempt by Gandhi and other nineteenth century contributions must be taken seriously and incorporated into any similar attempt to assess Indian philosophy in its current state.

The last part also has two chapters. Both chapters critically examine the attempts to absorb Buddhism into Hinduism. The first chapter presents a critique of Ananda K. Coomaraswamy, whose cultural nationalism seeks to co-opt Buddhism as part of Hinduism, by providing a common cultural and aesthetic heritage for the two. While presenting internationalism as the core of Indian nationalism, he draws his resources from the Asoka period, but credits Hinduism with having provided them. Similarly, the next chapter in this part discusses S. Radhakrishnan, who also explains away the radical project of Buddha and Buddhism, and portrays it as part of Hinduism. This move brings into the discussion Ambedkar, who bolsters the differences between Buddhism and Hinduism, and T. R. V. Murti, who highlights the mutual influences across the two philosophical systems.

Thus, this book brings to bear critical perspectives on some of the major Indian philosophers' discussions on the West, modernity, colonialism, classical Indian philosophy, and modern Western philosophy. The critical evaluation of the works of these prominent philosophers will enable us to take stock of the strengths, while also making us aware of the limitations, or even weaknesses, that prevail in the practice of philosophy in India. This distance between the expected and the actual state of affairs, with respect to Indian philosophy, can clarify methods of reinvigorating philosophical activity in India, thereby enabling it to undertake the larger tasks that Bhattacharyya apportioned to it. This will not only enrich the discipline but make the discipline fulfil its irreplaceable, and previously assigned, tasks.

There are works that deal with contemporary Indian philosophy, such as *Contemporary Indian Philosophy*, edited by S. Radhakrishnan and J. H. Muirhead (1952), *Spirit of Modern India*, edited by Robert A. McDermott and V. S. Naravane (2010), and *Indian Philosophy in English: From Renaissance to Independence*, edited by Nalini Bhushan and Jay L. Garfield (2011). These make contemporary writing in Indian philosophy available to a modern audience. As a means of advancing beyond what is already available, this book makes a critical evaluation of contemporary Indian philosophers. While identifying how contemporary Indian philosophers re-wrote their ancestors, and responded to outsiders, this work identifies important themes that philosophy in India might take up for further discussion, and thereby extend its purview while enriching its resources. This stock-taking of the contribution of contemporary Indian philosophers belonging to the twentieth century will enable us to establish a productive and creative relationship between India and philosophy, thereby preparing the ground for 'discovering the soul of India', as envisaged by Bhattacharyya.

There are some inevitable repetitions that I have retained, in the hope that instead of making the reading monotonous, they work like the chorus in a song or the thread in a garland of flowers, to sustain continuity with reminders.

I

Indian Solutions to Western Problems

1

ADVAITA TO KANT

This is a story about Guru Paramanandayya and his disciples. Ten of his disciples went to the forest to collect firewood. On their way back they lost their way and had to cross a river, in full spate. After crossing it they wanted to make sure that all ten of them had crossed the river. One started counting but got only nine. Finding one missing, he began to worry. Then, each disciple began counting but each found only nine. They were all worried that one of their members was missing. They ran to their Guru and reported that one disciple was missing. The Guru asked them all to stand in a row, and found all ten there. And the disciples were happy. (Folk tale from south India)

K ant is one of the pre-eminent bonesetters history has produced. If we accept that it was Descartes who, in formulating the project of modernity, removed everything of the pre-modern and retained only the skeleton in the form of a bare and brittle cogito, then it was Hume who broke the spine of this skeleton. However, it was Kant who healed the broken bones. He was an important Enlightenment thinker. We may remember that post-modern philosophers like Foucault found it necessary to discuss Kant seriously, especially in the essay 'What Is Enlightenment' (1984). Feminists like S. M. Okin in her essay 'Reason and Feeling in Thinking about Justice' (1989) trace the gender bias in modern political philosophy, particularly in the writings of John Rawls, to its participation in the Kantian legacy. That is, although Descartes is the founder of the Enlightenment, it is in Kant that it becomes socially and ethically more responsible.

While there is a totally radical position taken by Descartes in his formulation of the project of Enlightenment or of modernity, this posture turns out to be too abstract. Alternatively, while the project of Enlightenment is wholly radical, in Kant it becomes more responsible. For instance, the autonomous self in Kant does become responsible to other autonomous selves, thus paving the way for inter-subjectivity, or for later developments in Hegel and other phenomenological thinkers. Without Kant, Western philosophy taking off from Descartes would not have expanded as it later did. It might have ended with a whimper. It is this that makes Kant's contribution to the project of modernity significant, whose impact has not been confined to its place of origin, but spread like wildfire across the globe, affecting India as well. Aside from this macro-level influence, Kant is important to India in another respect, this time in a specific and academic sense. A contemporary Indian philosopher, Krishna Chandra Bhattacharyya, explicitly bases his philosophical analysis on a critique of Kant.

In this chapter, I shall briefly discuss Bhattacharyya's critique of Kant, focusing on his work, 'The Concept of Philosophy.'[1] Following this, the chapter will present Bhattacharyya's critique of Indian solutions to the Kantian problem. In this context, I argue that instead of travelling in space, an activity fraught with many problems of cultural translation, there is a need to travel in time. In this process, the chapter also points out the disguised divinity that persists in Kant and offers traditional Western solutions to modern Western problems.

While both Western and Indian classical philosophies have accepted the idea of an agentless consciousness or divine consciousness, this chapter discusses the problems associated with the relation between self as a knower and the unknowability of self or self-knowledge. It will focus on two primary aspects of this, self-knowledge, and certainty, to help clarify the Kantian problematic. The Kantian problematic, for Bhattacharyya, lies in the 'knowability of the self as a metaphysical entity.' Kant makes self the source of knowledge but Bhattacharyya says self 'is not in itself knowable.' Kant postulates the unknowability of the self in order to avoid a logical impasse. That is, if self is knowable then that self needs to be known; this in turn has to be known by something else, and this goes on towards an infinite regression.[2] In order to avoid this predicament, Bhattacharyya argues, Kant justifies his choice by making self a 'necessity of thought' and an 'object of moral faith' (1983: 462).

Moving forward from Bhattacharyya's diagnosis we can show the Kantian justification to be a weak justification for establishing the existence of self, particularly, when self is the central or key concept in modern Western philosophy. Bhattacharyya claims that making 'thinking' as equivalent to 'knowing' in Kant is responsible for the agnosticism.[3] He alleges that it is this equating of 'thinking' and 'knowing' which underlies the Kantian problematic.[4] Bhattacharyya's diagnosis of the Kantian problematic is novel. Other philosophers, such as Brentano, Menong, and Husserl, who largely toed the Hegelian line in understanding and overcoming the Kantian problematic, have not seen this problem in Kant the way that Bhattacharyya did. They tried to overcome the problem by naturalizing the self or offering formulations such as 'being-in-the-world', *a la* Heidegger. Apart from these developments within the phenomenological tradition, within the analytical tradition, it has been sought to overcome the solipsism of the modern self through Wittgenstein's well-known thesis of ordinary language argument.

Bhattacharyya approaches Kant differently. His ingenuity lies in his ability to use the Advaitic position, or its insights, to understand the Kantian problematic, through a critical comparison. In this way, he becomes a fine and fitting example of his own observation in his famous essay 'Svaraj in Ideas', where he talks of contributing to a culturally informed understanding of Indian thinkers in the context of their reading of texts from other cultures. He says—

> One would have expected after a century of contact with the vivifying ideas of the west that there should be vigorous output of Indian contribution in a distinctive Indian style to the culture and thought of modern world,—contribution specially to humane subjects like history, philosophy or literature, a contribution such as may be enjoyed by our countrymen who still happen to retain their vernacular mind

and which might be recognized by others as reflecting the distinctive soul of India. Barring the contribution of a few men of genius—and genius is largely independent of the times—there is not much evidence of such creative work done by our educated men. (1984: 385)

In my assessment, Bhattacharyya is no doubt among those few men in whose writings the 'distinctive soul of India' has been reflected. Now let us discuss his offer of Advaitic solutions to the Kantian problematic. Bhattacharyya points to the need to break open the equivalence between 'knowing' and 'thinking' assumed by Kant, and suggests that in addition to thinking there are ways of knowing outside the mode of thinking. To quote him—'My position is ... that the self is unthinkable and on the other that while actually it is not known and is only an object of faith, though not necessarily only of moral faith, we have to admit the possibility of knowing it without *thinking*...' (1983: 462).

At the outset, let me point out that Bhattacharyya's position is closer to the Advaita position, if not Advaita *per se*.[5] In elucidating this 'knowing without thinking', he distinguishes four grades of thought.

Four Grades of Thought

(*a*) Empirical Thought (ET): Empirical thought is the theoretical consciousness of a content involving reference to an object that is perceived or imagined to be perceived.

(*b*) Pure Objective Thought (POT): Pure objective thought refers to contents that are objects but have no necessary reference to sense-perception. He also calls this 'contemplative thought'.

(*c*) Spiritual Thought (ST): The contents of spiritual thought are no objects; nothing that is contemplated here is in the objective attitude. It is subjective, in the sense of being appreciated in a subjective or 'enjoying' attitude.

(*d*) Transcendental Thought (TT): Transcendental thought is the consciousness of a content that is neither objective nor subjective. In Bhattacharyya's reckoning, Transcendental truth is that aspect of thought which is knowledge, which is, strictly speaking, not thinking but beyond thought. This is also the domain of truth. He says of the absolute—

> The absolute as transcending the enjoyed reality of religion is positive being (truth) or positive non-being (freedom) or their positive indetermination (value). The absolute is conceived rigorously as truth in (Advaita) Vedānta. What is loosely called nihilist Buddhism apparently understands the absolute as freedom. The Hegelian absolute may be taken to represent the indetermination, miscalled *identity* of truth and freedom which is value. All these views belong to what may be called the transcendental grades of philosophy. (1983: 478–9)

Although Bhattacharyya also refers to nihilist Buddhism and Hegel, I will not discuss them here, since his central focus is Advaita and the other two schools are used primarily to further illustrate his point about truth. Having distinguished four grades of thought, Bhattacharyya also describes ET as Fact, POT as Self-subsistent, ST as Reality, and TT as Truth. He classifies these under two broad categories, namely, the domain of science and the domain of philosophy. He places fact under science and the other three, Self-subsistence, Reality, and Truth, under philosophy. Specifying the major differences between these two broad domains, which he sharply demarcates, Bhattacharyya explains that fact is spoken of as information and understood without reference to a spoken form. It need not be spoken to be believed because speakability is a contingent character of the content of ET. In sharp contrast, speakability is a 'necessary character of the content of pure philosophic thought.' In addition, speaking is not merely speaking as information and all speech is not expressed in the form of judgments. Even in those cases where thoughts are expressed in the form of a judgment, it [speaking] is only artificial and symbolic. Referring to the spoken, which necessarily refers to the speaking of it, there are three forms, respectively as it is spoken in the objective, subjective, or in the transcendental attitude.

Correspondingly, there are four grades of speakables. Like the different grades of thought, Bhattacharyya makes a general distinction between science and philosophy with reference to speakability. He says that the contents of fact are spoken as information and are intelligible without reference to the speaking of it, whereas the contents of philosophy are not spoken as information and they are necessarily dependent on the speaking. Elucidating different grades of speakability, he says that in the factual domain, that is, ET, in the statement, 'x is', 'x', 'is', and their combination are literal. In POT, 'x' is literal, 'is' is literal, but not their combination, which is symbolic. In ST, 'x' is literal, 'is' and their combination are symbolic. In TT, 'x', 'is', and their combination are all symbolic.

Thus, by distinguishing four grades of thought he shows how knowing consists of not only thinking but also non-thinking knowledge. That is, there is a non-cognitive source of knowledge by way of aesthetic and spiritual knowledge (or self-knowledge), which also constitutes the knowledge domain. This eluded the attention of Kant, forcing his relapse into agnosticism. Therefore, this non-cognitive knowledge can save the Kantian self from agnosticism.

The two important aspects of Bhattacharyya's engagement with Kant are—his critique of Kant and his Advaitic solution to the Kantian problem. While holding Bhattacharyya's critique of Kant in high regard, let me however add a caveat, namely, that there is a problem associated with Bhattacharyya, particularly in his attempt at fashioning a mode, or participating in an already existing fashion, in which Indian solutions are offered for Western problems. This, wittingly or unwittingly, makes the West a reservoir of problems and, correspondingly, the East, or India, a reservoir of solutions. More specifically, this merely inverts the view, which at the structural level was authored by the colonial discourse, in which India is the reservoir of problems and the West, that of solutions. What I find problematic is not so much the question of who is the reservoir of what but the very binary that underlies this formulation.

Here, let me digress a bit and point out that there are a number of resemblances between Gandhi and Bhattacharyya; for instance, their rejection of positing a continuity between matter and spirit, or materialism and spiritualism. That is, unlike positing the continuity between science and spiritualism, or matter and spirit, as conjectured by Swami Vivekananda and Sri Aurobindo, Bhattacharyya is in the company of Gandhi in rejecting any such continuity. Moreover, and more importantly, Gandhi and Bhattacharyya have each authored a text bearing the word *Swaraj* in its name, *Hind Swaraj* by Gandhi and 'Svaraj in Ideas' by Bhattacharyya. Additionally, both Bhattacharyya and Gandhi are influenced by Jainism.

Notwithstanding these entrenched resemblances, to return to the specific question of offering Indian solutions to Western problems, Bhattacharyya is in the company of Swami Vivekananda and Sri Aurobindo, and not with Gandhi. The latter, unlike Bhattacharyya, generally refrained from using remedies from across the culture at the outset. For instance, Gandhi would see spiritual Christianity as a solution to the material West, not Advaita or yoga, from India. Conversely, he would find internal resources to overcome or eliminate evils in Indian society, like untouchability or problems relating to caste. At a more general level, he would find in these remedies from across cultural borders, a tendency to deflect the interiority and internal preoccupations of individuals within the community.[6] Here I am not suggesting that Gandhi was a cultural puritan, but making a plea for taking his metaphor of a house with open windows, seriously. For Gandhi, remedies from the other cultures, if sought, must first be diligently deliberated. Such an action should also be preceded by a thorough search for internal remedies, and only if they are not found, can one then turn to remedies from outside. Such remedies need also to be sensitive to cultural differences, and one must be as cautious in selecting them as in choosing a blood group for transfusion.

While noting these differences between Gandhi and Bhattacharyya, it is necessary to remember that the latter, in his eagerness to propose an Advaitic solution to overcome Kant's problematic, does not sufficiently emphasize interesting and important details made available by his diagnosis of Kant. Thus, Bhattacharyya traverses a spatially distinct philosophical school, namely, Advaita. In this chapter, I want, instead, to reopen a route in a temporal terrain, to relate Kant to theology in the West, and, similarly, to shift the ground of our discussion from epistemology to metaphysics or ontology. For instance, the Kantian self is surrounded by theological or metaphysical aspects in disguise. That is, Kant is trying to embellish self with the aspects associated with divinity in Classical thought, which they rejected, at one level, installing the self in its place. That is, God is rejected, and in His place, the self is installed. Like God, who is a creator but is not created, the self in Kant is the knower, but cannot be known. It is my contention that while the European Enlightenment claimed to be radical in rejecting tradition, some crucial aspects of tradition have sneaked back in, either surreptitiously or because of the somnolence of modernity. Further, there seems to be specificity in this sneaking back, which makes us reconsider modernity's claims of success in its assault upon tradition.[7] In order to distinguish this specificity, let me recall two important and profound cautions against complacency with regard to the disappearance of the past, by Althusser (1984) and Ronald Barthes (1997). In his well-known piece titled 'Ideology and Ideological State Apparatuses', Althusser writes—'Even after a social revolution like that of 1917, a large part of the State apparatus survived after the seizure of State power by the alliance of the proletariat and the small peasantry: Lenin repeated the fact again and again' (1984: 14–15).

Similarly, we have Barthes who reminds us, or we may conclude from his essay 'The Death of the Author', that God as the creator of the world is replaced by the author as the sole creator of the text. Taking cue from these thinkers, I want to explore those aspects of tradition which seem to have survived the onslaught of modernity. Taking Althusser's caution against complacency seriously, I want to explore some similarities between traditional philosophy and Kant. In this context, let me put forward a classical argument for the existence of God. Offering proof for the existence of God, Thomas Aquinas writes—

> It is therefore impossible that in the same respect and in the same way a thing should be both mover and moved, i.e., that it should move itself. Therefore, whatever is in motion must be put in motion by another. If that by which it is put in motion be itself put in motion,

then this also must needs be put in motion by another, and that by another again. But this cannot go on to infinity, because then there would be no first mover, and, consequently, no other mover; seeing that subsequent movers move only inasmuch as they are put in motion by the first mover; as the staff moves only because it is put in motion by the hand. Therefore it is necessary to arrive at a first mover, put in motion by no other; and this everyone understands to be God.[8]

Like the Kantian self, which is the only repository of knowledge, knowing the outside reality, God, in theology, is the mover and cannot be said to move. Just as the effort to know the Kantian self leads to an infinite regression, so too the effort to move the divine being relapses into an infinite regression. So, similar to the requirement to 'arrive at a first mover, put in motion by no other; and this everyone understands to be God', there is in Kant too the self which is the knower but which is not known. In this respect, the problems of theology are not significantly different from those that are faced by Kant.

Taking our cue from Bhattacharyya, or to extrapolate from his insights, we can deduce that the problem with the Kantian self is its unknowability, which is an epistemological problem, but its autonomy is a metaphysical problem. The Kantian self is unknowable because it is autonomous and not vice versa. That is, autonomy of the self is the constitutive aspect in Kant. Since it is autonomous and not dependent, it is the source of knowledge but cannot be known. There is a complex continuity and a discontinuity underlying this. The discontinuity lies in the fact that, unlike the classical notion of self that is dependent on either nature or divinity, the modern self, beginning from Descartes, is autonomous. In this sense, it is a radical departure from the classical framework. However, there is a surreptitious continuity that haunts the modern self, namely, that its autonomy shows major shades of classical divinity. Just as God is the source of knowledge in Classical theory, and man only participates in the divine discourse, similarly in the modern theories, God is dispensed with, and in His place an autonomous self is installed with the same kind of omnipotence. It is this metaphysical move that creates the epistemological problem in Kant. The autonomous self comes to be constituted more prominently by Descartes. But this autonomous self is not to be equated with the empirical self. The autonomous self is endowed with divine qualities and is human only in name.

Thus, we can understand Kant through this Cartesian legacy. The Cartesian self, though reductionist, is, however, less vulnerable to inconsistencies. It is Kant who in the process of naturalizing the Cartesian self makes it vulnerable to criticism, such as that made by Bhattacharyya. This move by Kant, to naturalize the autonomous self, haunts the later Western philosophy of Hegel, Minong, Husserl, Sartre, and others. For these philosophers, the transcendental status of self becomes enigmatic but indispensable. Husserl and Sartre tried to dispense with it but finally had to accept it. Viewed from this perspective, the quest for certainty is more a theological and classical quest than scientific. Further, the achievement of modernity is confined, to use Althusser's insight, to the removal of agency, in this case, God, and installing in its place the human, without destroying the structures inhabited by the erstwhile agency, that is, God. Here, one starts wondering whether what Bhattacharyya is alluding to is the presence of the Guru in the story mentioned earlier, an appeal that obviates a return to the classical theories. It is against this backdrop that one has to re-examine the relation between modernity and tradition today. It is like the self looking at the mirror to see its own reflection. So Kant faced these problems because he instituted an autonomous self, and attributes to it those divine characteristics which make it omnipotent and in a changed context differently vulnerable.

Further, we can also detect in the modern quest for self an obsession with certain knowledge (see Raghuramaraju 2005). That is, there seems to be an inconsistency between finite human subjects and certain knowledge. Taking those aspects generally associated with God or divinity in the Classical period, such as the unknowability of God, or the quest for certainty, Kant embellishes the self with them. In this changed scenario, the modern self does not become a natural and empirical individual, or his or her ally, but threatens to show its proximity to the divine, which is at the root of modern anthropocentrism, a threat to ordinary empirical human beings.[9]

Thus, notwithstanding the radical posture of the project of modernity, some crucial aspects of the tradition which they claimed to have rejected, survived, at least in a disguised form. Recognizing the features that survived is not only important for those who inhabit modernity, since such a recognition would make them more cautious and less complacent, but also those who critique modernity, as this would save them from offering remedies from distant social spaces when temporal and local ones are available.

To come back to the main point, the problem with Bhattacharyya's attempt is that he tries to solve an ontological problem at an epistemological level. That is, self in Kant is unknowable which is similar to that of the unmover in theology—the unmover in theology makes sense even though we may not accept it, but the unknower in modernity is embarrassing, as it smacks of the divinity which has been discarded. Instead of revealing the divine aspects in Kant, Bhattacharyya enters into negotiating the problem at an epistemological level, where he proposes to broaden it by including non-thinking as part of knowing. That is, this broadened knowledge proposed by Bhattacharyya culminates in the empirical self, which passes through the four stages suggested by him, ultimately becoming divine. Alternatively, it may be postulated that the self at TT does not remain an empirical self but becomes a transcendental self or over-personal self, which is a form of divinity. If this is granted then, rather than routing the Kantian problematic through Advaita and thus traversing distant cultures, all in order to achieve or face divinity, I suggest it to be recognized that this divinity already exists within Western thought, and in theology.

It is this disguised theology in Kant that eluded the attention of Bhattacharyya, which interests me enormously. It is perhaps this counting self (in the story given at the beginning of this chapter) or the knowing self, which is not counted or known, that is needed. Moreover, there is a need to bring back the Divine self. That is, while Bhattacharyya attempts to humanize the Kantian self, I want to disclose its divine aspects, thereby neutralizing the radical stance in Kant. This makes Bhattacharyya's critique of Kant redundant, robbing the

Kantian self with traditional dress. Thus, unlike Bhattacharyya who tries to Indianize the Kantian self, I want to classicalize it. While Bhattacharyya's attempt traverses space, mine traverses time. In other words, I argue, there is a need to broaden the terms of Kantian problematic to include theology. Without paying attention to these significant developments taking place within Western philosophy, I am afraid, it would be rash to make a sudden jump, lest 'the jump' remain uninformed of the complexities discussed earlier.

Let me summarize my arguments: While accepting the novelty of Bhattacharyya's critique of the Kantian problematic, I pointed out the problem in his solution, that is, his offering of an Advaitic solution. Instead, I have shown that there is a need to disclose the divinity that is disguised in Kant and take him back in time to the traditional discourses of theology and frameworks that include divinity. In this process, I also clarified the shift from metaphysics to epistemology, which eluded Bhattacharyya's analysis.

My purpose in this chapter has been to read carefully the comparative axis, thereby avoiding both mere dismissal, and an uncritical celebration of these scholarly criticisms on Western philosophy by contemporary Indian philosophers. This is important because such critical writings carry either wittingly or otherwise essential cultural colourings. However, when discovering such colourings and admiring its brilliance, one must be vigilant about the gaps and lapses, or glosses, that might have caused many not to take these writings seriously. One way of making these contemporary Indian metaphysical writings available to the community of philosophers is to read them seriously. The next chapter discusses another, though different example, where Akeel Bilgrami offers another Indian, Mahatma Gandhi, as an alternative to the problems of Western moral philosophy.

Notes

1. The reason why I have focussed on Krishna Chandra Bhattacharyya's essay 'The Concept of Philosophy', and not his book *The Subject as*

Freedom, is that this essay represents his mature philosophy. Pointing out the differences between *The Subject as Freedom* and 'The Concept of Philosophy', Kalidas Bhattacharyya says—

> These are not difficult theses for those who are acquainted with Bhattacharyya's *The Subject as Freedom*. But there are some additional points— some of which bear even adversely on what he has said in that monograph—which ought to be noted immediately.
>
> First, there is no significant reference, in that monograph, and certainly too no elaboration of it, either to pure self-subsistent object or to pure objective thought or the exact status of metaphysics (and logic) and their relation, on the other hand, to empirical object and empirical thought and, on the other hand, to pure subjectivity and spiritual philosophy…. He has rather shown how directly from science we turn to this latter. Metaphysics, undenied, has not been paid even a fraction of attention he pays to it in his *The Concept of Philosophy*….
>
> Secondly, what he writes, in this essay, on pure spiritual thinking and its content is not only an improvement, in certain fundamentals, on what he has said on (spiritual) introspection in his *The Subject as Freedom*….
>
> Thirdly, while in *The Subject as Freedom* Bhattacharyya placed the stage 'beyond introspection' under the class *spiritual subjectivity*, here in his *The Concept of Philosophy* he understands the *absolute* as the content of a grade of thought which is *no longer spiritual*, the reason being that the content here – the absolute – has primarily to be called truth rather than reality and truth is as much qualitatively distinct from reality as reality from self-subsistent object: while reality is all subjective, truth is neither subjective nor objective. (1975: 187–92)

This is the reason why I discussed his essay. I also find his 2011 work not saying anything new.

2. There is an instance in the *Brihad-Āranyaka* Upanishad which is reminiscent of this situation, when Gārgī asks—

> "'On what then, pray, are the worlds of Brahma woven, warp and woof?'"
>
> Yājñavalkya said: "Gārgī, do not question too much, lest your head fall off. In truth, you are questioning too much about a divinity about which further questions cannot be asked. Gārgī, do not over-question.'" (Hume, 2003: 114)

3. Here, it may be noted that Bhattacharyya points out yet another problem or lapse in Kant when he says—

> In taking the self to be unthinkable, I understand Kant's idea of the Reason to be not only not knowledge, but to be not even thought in the

literal sense. The so-called extension of thought beyond experience and the possibility of experience means to me only the use of the verbal form of thought as a symbol of an unthinkable reality, such symbolising use not being thinking. (1983: 462)

4. It is possible that Kant has not made the mistake that is pointed out by Krishna Chandra Bhattacharyya.

5. Similar to Bhattacharyya, R. D. Ranade too traces this problem in Kant to Upanishads. He says—

   Epistemologically, we are told in various passages of the Upanisads, it would not be possible for us to know the Self in the technical meaning of the word "knowledge". Our readers might bring to mind the fact that Kant equally well regarded Reality, as consisting of God and the Self, as technically unknowable. These were, he said, merely matters of faith. The Upanisadic answer is that it is true that God and the Self are unknowable, but they are not merely objects of faith, they are objects of mystical realization. Then, again, the Upanisads do not regard the Self as unknowable in the agnostic sense of the word, for example, in the sense in which Spencer understands it. Rather, it is "unknowable" from the standpoint of philosophic humility. (in Bhushan and Garfield 2011: 263)

   Swami Vivekananda too, distinguishes unknowability in agnostics from Advaitic. He says—'But what Advaita says is that God is more than knowable. This is a great fact to learn. You must not go home with the idea that God is unknowable in the sense in which agnostics put it.... God is more than known' (in Bhushan and Garfield 2011: 315).

6. See also Basham, A. L., in Ravindra Kumar (ed.), 1971.

7. Here I am deliberately using the word tradition and not pre-modern as the latter is a larger reality and more difficult to combat than perhaps the former is.

8. Aquinas, St. Thomas. 1920. *The Summa Theologica of St. Thomas Aquinas*. Second and Revised Edition, literally translated by Fathers of the English Dominican Province. Online Edition Copyright © 2003 by Kevin Knight.

9. However, it must be recognized that this garb is removed only in the liberals, who, through the method of induction, rejected the certainty of knowledge and naturalized the self and morality.

2

GANDHI TO WESTERN MORAL PHILOSOPHY

This chapter discusses another instance of offering Indian solutions to Western problems. However, here, what is offered is not taken from classical Indian philosophy but from Mahatma Gandhi, of modern India. This chapter focuses on Akeel Bilgrami's famous essay titled 'Gandhi's Integrity: The Philosophy behind the Politics' (2006). Summarizing the history of moral philosophy in the West, Bilgrami writes that choosing an 'action on moral grounds under certain circumstances is to generate a principle which we think applied as an "ought" or an imperative to *all* others faced with relevantly similar circumstances' (2006: 255). This entire tradition that equates morality with moral principles was, according to Bilgrami, repudiated by Gandhi, who set up a thorough-going alternative to the concept of principle in moral philosophy. Having made this point about Gandhi, Bilgrami goes on to elaborate various important aspects of Gandhi's moral philosophy. Here, it is important to note that the very structure of Bilgrami's essay, particularly the tone as well as the volume of discussion, tends to push the reader towards those wonderful novel ideas about Gandhi brought for the first time into the mainstream. That is, by its nature, the structure of the essay takes the reader to the alternative to Western moral philosophy. This, it can be argued, does not then allow the reader to see important aspects which are essential to understanding the significance of the essay. Going against the grain of existing emphasis and the tone of the essay, it is necessary to read it more carefully and identify its different parts to decipher different significances underlying it. This essay can be said to consist of three important aspects—

(1) Though brief, there is an attempt to present in a summary form the very nerve centre of moral philosophy in the West. That is, Western moral philosophy is equated here with moral principles. There is a need to critically assess this summary in order to get at the root of Bilgrami's analysis. In order to do this, it is necessary to take a fresh look at the major changes in the history of Western moral philosophy.

(2) Having identified this essential aspect of the West, Bilgrami goes on to contrast this with Gandhi's moral philosophy, namely, the moral philosopher as an exemplar. Identifying the exemplar helps Bilgrami to avoid the inherent problems of universalizability, though not universalism.

(3) The third important aspect of Bilgrami's essay is its clarification of how reading Gandhi—along the lines of Western moral philosophy as has been undertaken by Sumit Sarkar—is a spectacular misreading.

It is necessary to return to these aspects of Bilgrami's essay and subject them to a close reading. There is a tendency to take the latter two aspects more seriously and gloss over the first one. This can become a problem and will not enable the reader to recognize some crucial elements of the essay. As already indicated, the first aspect seeks to present the essential nature, and even the common assumptions of Western moral philosophy. The assessment, presented briefly here, can be treated as an axiom on which the whole edifice of the essay rests. It is necessary to unpack this axiom and subject it to a critical examination.

Bilgrami makes a distinction between universality and universalizability. He characterizes the former as suggesting that 'a moral value, whether or not someone in particular holds it, applies to all persons'. On the other hand, the latter requires that, 'if someone in particular holds a moral value, then *he* must think that it applies to all others...' (2006: 255). Hence, while universality in this particular definition makes morality independent or autonomous of practitioners, universalizability, on the other hand, invariably demands its acceptance by all. That is, it does not accept any variation between one person's acceptance of a moral principle and its lack of acceptance by others. It is this demand to universalize first-person moral values to the rest that Bilgrami identifies as engendering violence. Bilgrami explores the possibility of positing that something possesses universal moral value, and yet not demanding its universalizability. This is a challenging task for him as he finds universalizability to be pervasive in the 'long history in the Western tradition of moral philosophy' (2006: 255). This moral process, as already pointed out, contains in it elements of criticism, that is, the criticism of those who do not accept what you believe to be universal, which leads to the use of violence. However, if we remove universalizability, there is then the danger of moral solipsism via subjectivism.

It is at this juncture of opinions that Bilgrami finds in Gandhi a repudiation of this entire Western tradition and the proposition of a viable and radical alternative. Gandhi, claims Bilgrami, repudiated all of Western moral theory which is wedded to universalizability, and yet at the same time, did not encourage 'self-enclosed moral' subjectivism. He reconciled the rejection of the universalizability of a value's potential for being wielded in criticism of others with the yearning for one's choices to possess significance for others. He does this in the following way—while Western moral thinking maintains that—'"When one chooses for oneself, one chooses for everyone". The first half of the slogan describes a particular person's act of conscience. The second half of the slogan transforms the act of conscience to a universalized principle, an imperative which others must follow or be criticized' (2006: 257). Bilgrami points out that Gandhi accepts this kind of thinking too. However, Bilgrami considers that Gandhi 'understands the second half ... differently. He too wants one's acts of conscience to have a universal relevance, so he too thinks one chooses for everyone, but he does not see that as meaning that one generates a principle or imperative for everyone'. Rather, Bilgrami explicates the following bold proposal in Gandhi—'When one chooses for oneself *one sets an example to everyone*'. For Gandhi, the role of the *satyagrahi* is not to formulate principles from their moral conscience but to 'lead exemplary lives, to set examples to everyone by their actions'. This concept of the exemplar, contends Bilgrami, is 'a wholesale alternative to the concept of principle in moral philosophy' (2006: 257). This Gandhian alternative, Bilgrami further claims, while it retains what is right by Mill, namely, the importance of being modest in one's moral opinions, it rejects what is unsatisfactory by Mill. In Gandhi's case, since no principle is generated,

> it puts us in no position to be critical of others because there is no *generality* in their truth, of which others may fall *afoul*. Others may not follow. Our example may not set. But that is not the same as disobeying an imperative, violating a principle. As a result, the entire moral psychology of our response to others who depart from us is necessarily much weaker. At the most we may be disappointed in others that they will not follow our example, and at least part of the disappointment is in ourselves that our example has not taken hold. And the critical point is that disappointment is measurably weaker than criticism, it is not the paler shade of contempt, hostility and eventual violence. (2006: 258)

To begin with, while Western morality has predominantly proposed various moral principles, it must, however, be pointed out that this fails to take note of some important exceptions. For instance, it is philosophically viable to grant that mainstream moral philosophy in the West is privileged, or even, as pointed out by Bilgrami, preoccupied with moral principles. However, here we cannot forget two important moral agents who are exemplars in Bilgrami's definition of that concept—Socrates and Jesus Christ. Plato's Socrates may be offering moral principles. However, the very life of Socrates too is effective, perhaps more effective than the principles attributed to him by Plato. It is hardly possible to think of the impact of Plato's thought or even of Greek moral thought as a whole on subsequent civilizations without the example of the life of Socrates, particularly his trial and death. Bereft of this, mere moral principles would remain weak and ineffective. The success of Greek moral thought is closely intertwined with the example of Socrates' life; the latter aspect overtakes the former.

In addition to the life of Socrates, let us look at his moral philosophy. One of his central arguments is the refusal to accept weakness of will, *akrasia* or moral error in the domain of morality. He argued that knowing something to be true is to follow it. At the outset, he ruled out the possibility of someone knowing something to be true yet not practising it. For him, on the other hand, not practising the truth meant, by definition, that that person did not know what was true. This principle ensures that there cannot be any variance or discrepancy between knowing and doing. The moral principle of an agent invariably demands of him or her to be an exemplar. So this is surely a further instance of the availability of a moral exemplar in the Western tradition that eluded the attention of Bilgrami.[1]

Now, let me turn to another important moral exemplar in the West—Jesus Christ. The life of Christ and the moral principles derived from it have also played a vital role in shaping Western moral theory. Even those who reject its theology, as Russell did, concede the impact of its moral theory on people. Leaving aside the justification of Christian morality, what cannot be denied is the tremendous impact it has and continues to have on Western society. This is despite the success of modernity, which is at loggerheads with Christianity. Christ too fits Bilgrami's definition of exemplars but once again, Bilgrami fails to take note of this. On careful reading, it is this idea of setting the example, rather than the concept of universalizability, that seems to have been at the core of Christ's intervention when he told the mob gathered around a woman accused of adultery, that he who was sinless amongst them should cast the first stone. Rather than demanding universalizability, he was, I think, asking people to set an example and not become mere implementers

of moral principles. Bilgrami's reference in this essay to Christian
ethics is in the context of the similarity between Christian thought
and Kantian moral philosophy. He writes—

> It is a commonplace in our understanding of the Western moral
> tradition to think of Kant's moral philosophy as a full and *philosophi-
> cal* flowering of a core of Christian thought. But Gandhi fractures
> that historical understanding. By stressing the deep incompatibility
> between categorical imperative and universalizable maxims on the
> one hand, and Christian humility on the other, he makes two moral
> doctrines and methods out of what the tradition represents as a single
> historically consolidated one. (2006: 258)

That is, in his preoccupation with setting up Gandhian moral thought
against all of Western moral thinking, Bilgrami fails to recognize
those dominant aspects in the West which might be used as internal
resources to provide a contrast with what he rightly identified as the
dominant obsession with the West, namely dispensing principles.

Therefore, both Greek thought as dominated by Socrates, and
Christianity, remain outside Bilgrami's reckoning in his assessment
of Western moral philosophy. Yet, the lives of these two influential
moralists surely fit into the idea of exemplar. If this is accepted, what
can be further considered is whether these two are different types of
exemplars from that which Gandhi is. That is, first there is a need
to recognize that both Socrates and Christ are exemplars. If they are
not, this needs to be demonstrated. If they are, yet are different from
Gandhi, this variance too needs to be argued for. More importantly,
there is a need to clarify the concept of exemplar, render it as a larger
category, and relegate Gandhi to the representation of one example
of this larger category. Otherwise, as it stands, there is a danger of
taking the category of exemplars and Gandhi as identical.

In order to facilitate a further discussion on this issue, we need
to open it up for discussion and assess the philosophical viability of
the lives of Socrates and Christ. Take a careful second look at the
relation between the knowledge of truth and practicing it, following
Socrates' philosophy. Ascertain whether these two Western moral

figures are exemplars. If they are, then are they similar or different from Gandhi? This can result in the serious consideration of important issues which have been left out by Bilgrami. As it stands, there is a discrepancy between Western moral philosophy and the domains that Bilgrami covers under this heading. This makes his conclusion unwieldy even if one follows the inductive process to arrive at the conclusion. This is because of the possible counter examples available which have been pointed out. However, modern Western moral theory is predominantly obsessed with moral principles. This is also evident from the arguments cited by Bilgrami. Mill, Austin, Hare, and others that he brings into discussion, are all modern Western moral philosophers. There is no mention of Plato, Aristotle, or St. Augustine, for example, in the essay.

This vast glossing over by Bilgrami is part of a larger theoretical terrain inhabited by post-colonialism and championed by Edward Said. It appears that Bilgrami is working within this terrain. Said, in his influential book *Orientalism* (1979), discusses modern figures like Carlyle and Mill but does not discuss the classical thinkers. Yet he seeks to generate from these a larger category called the West, which he contrasts with the East. (For more on this see my 2005a). This imbalance makes the conclusions problematic. They do not allow us to recognize the internal tensions between modernity in the West and its pre-modern tradition. It also does not let us recognize the internal resources available in the West to counter the tradition of issuing moral principles. This practice, of searching for alternatives from other traditions before searching within one's own, can become a serious problem. More importantly, such a move might be un-Gandhian. Gandhi largely avoided offering Indian solutions to Western problems. All major contemporary Indian thinkers, in one way or another, have given in to this temptation. Some glaring examples include Bankim Chandra, Swami Vivekananda, Sri Aurobindo, and even Krishna Chandra Bhattacharyya. In contrast, Gandhi largely advocated looking within one's own tradition. Yet, he was not an essentialist or a purist. He borrowed ideas that he considered necessary, which were unavailable in his own tradition, from outside.

Two important examples of such borrowing are pointed out by A. L. Basham—the celebration of manual labour which Gandhi took from Christianity and placing a high value on the role of women in society, which he also borrowed from the West (1971: 42). However, in his case, borrowing is preceded by an internal search. A central problem in Bilgrami's representation of a Gandhian alternative to the entire tradition of Western moral philosophy is that it counter poses, at least implicitly, Socrates and Christ with Gandhi. Placing Gandhi in their company adds to his stature.

Another difficulty with counter-alternatives from other cultures arises from the fact that they tread the same path, that of colonialism. Colonialism, as pointed out in the previous chapter, thrived on the formula that India was the repository of problems, and the West, the repository of solutions. In inverted form, this would present the West as the repository of problems and Gandhi from India as the repository of solutions. Imagine the case, if colonialism, having identified problems in India, suggested the search for internal resources before it offered those from the West—then it would not be colonialism. It is this theoretical burden, which unwittingly makes us participate in the theoretical terrain of colonialism, and which perhaps made Gandhi wary of the temptation of borrowing from outside, at the outset. Bilgrami could take a similar route out of the Saidian legacy and make a claim from such a position of externality.

There is yet another problem with Bilgrami's use of exemplar. This has to do with the flexibility of the exemplar. It is true that moral principles are—or at least tend to be—rigid. One part of this rigidity consists of universalizability, that is, moral principles do not give credence to difference and can encourage actions which may eventually erase difference. While this rigidity is problematic, and Bilgrami is right in pointing it out, one can see that flexibility in the exemplar may also become problematic, for different reasons. While agreeing with Bilgrami's preference for exemplary lives over moral principles, one might wonder how one accounts for morally wrong actions which also provide exemplars for others to emulate, using the provision of flexibility. In other words, Bilgrami seems to have considered only the good exemplars and left the discussion only half-complete. Alternatively, he seems to have taken into consideration only one aspect of exemplary life, namely, the good exemplars and not the bad exemplars. This might make his position on exemplary life, indirectly if not directly, vulnerable to his own powerful critique of liberalism, namely, an alcoholic asking for alcohol. Bilgrami may not be interested in providing a guarantee to prevent bad examples. However, if not a guarantee, we do need at least an example to prevent someone or something from becoming a bad example. At least we need a mechanism to contrast the bad from good, not necessarily negotiated through principles but through examples.

In addition to drawing the attention away from principles to the exemplar, in this context, there is a further need to recognize the importance of details and repetitions in 'moral-making'. While highlighting the effectiveness of the exemplar in smaller communities, Bilgrami rightly points out that Gandhi

> ... was fully aware that the smaller the community of individuals, the more likelihood there is of setting examples. In the context of family life, for example, one might see how parents by their actions may think or hope that they are setting examples to their children. Gandhi's ideal of peasant community organized in small *panchayat* or village units could perhaps at least approximate the family, where examples could be visibly set. That is, in part, why Gandhi strenuously argued that flows of populations to metropolis where there was far less scope for public perception of individual action, was destructive of moral life. (2006: 260)

Here it may be added that in addition to examples of small communities, parents and families play an important role by providing details and regular reminders about moral practices. Yet this facility of providing details and reminders is gradually becoming rare.

To sum up, this chapter underscores three important aspects of Bilgrami's essay. The chapter points out that the West has its own exemplars, such as Socrates and Jesus Christ, and that there is a need to actively consider such exemplars, thereby recognizing the presence of internal resources before looking to an external source, such as Gandhi. I find the call to begin to look at internal resources a more compelling message in Gandhi than the idea of the exemplar, which is undoubtedly given far greater importance in Bilgrami's portrayal.

This chapter and the previous one highlighted the underlying problems in two contemporary philosophers' attempts at providing Indian solutions to Western problems. I call this, following Delueze, the problem of excess or more. The next chapter discusses yet another instance, where an Indian resource is underspent to restore ethics to Indian philosophy, and bring it on par with Western moral philosophy. B. K. Matilal, while admitting that there is no moral philosophy in India that may be equated to Western moral philosophy, uses the epic Mahabharata to show the ethical dimension in Indian tradition, thereby making a claim of such equivalence. His attempt explicates the problem, which, in this case, is the problem of less.

Notes

1. To further understand these exceptions, there is a need to move away from Bilgrami and bring Foucault into the discussion. To understand better the location of Socrates' moral philosophy, it is necessary to analyse Foucault's interpretative critique of Kant. But before that, even at the cost of digression in order to merely find a point of reference for further analysis, let us record here that Aristotle, unlike Socrates, accepted the possibility of someone knowing what truth is without following it. Returning to Kant, he maintained that Enlightenment is an emancipatory project. There are two important concepts relating to our discussion in his famous prize-winning essay titled 'An Answer to the Question: "*What Is Enlightenment?*"' (Published on 30 September 1784 in Konigsberg, in Prussia). A central concept in this essay is, 'man's emergence from his self-incurred immaturity'. This immaturity, Kant clarifies, 'is the inability to use one's own understanding without the guidance of another'. Further, says Kant, this 'immaturity is *self-incurred* if its cause is not lack of understanding, but lack of resolution and courage to use it without the guidance of another'. Crystallizing the 'motto of enlightenment', Kant writes, 'Have courage to use your *own* understanding!' (1991: 54).

This was radical enough for many followers of Enlightenment and they did not ask for more. However, after nearly two centuries, Foucault did not think this was radical enough and he asked for more. This brings us to another aspect of Enlightenment explicated by Kant, namely, the distinction between 'the private and the public use of reason'. It is this distinction, rather than the earlier plea for the 'freedom of conscious-ness' that 'surprised' Foucault. This distinction confines the public use of reason only to 'understanding', without crossing over to political action. Kant held that the public domain is the domain of freedom whereas the private domain is duty bound. He says—

> The *public* use of man's reason must always be free, and it alone can bring about enlightenment among men; the *private use* of reason may quite often be very narrowly restricted, however, without undue hin-drance to the progress of enlightenment. But by the public use of one's own reason I mean that use which anyone may take of it *as a man of learning* addressing the entire *reading public*. What I term the private use of reason is that which a person may make of it in a particular *civil* post or office with which he is entrusted. (1991: 55)

This results in the moral maxim, '*Argue* as much as you like and about whatever you like, *but obey!*' In fact, we can here see the Cartesian con-nection in Kant. Descartes added a proviso to his radical claim of a com-plete rejection of anything, which is not reasoned. He says—

> Now before starting to rebuild your house, it is not enough to simply to pull it down, ... you must also provide yourself with some other place where you can live comfortably while building is in progress ... to obey the laws and customs of my country, holding constantly to the religion in which by God's grace I had been instructed from my childhood.... (1985: 122)

That is, Kant confined the terms of emancipation to understanding and freedom of expression, and simultaneously pleaded for the following of rules and adherence to duties. Though Kant's text is 'not capable of constituting an adequate description of Enlightenment,' says Foucault, 'Kant's reflections even a way of philosophizing that has not been without its importance or effectiveness during the last two centuries' (1984: 50).

Here, let me point out that although Foucault equates Kant's position on the Enlightenment with the view that he strictly confines the public use of reason to thought, without entering into the domain of action, he does concede the possibility of the public use of reason entering into the domain of political action. This is clear later in the essay, when he writes—

> Thus once the germ on which nature has lavished more care—man's inclination and vocation to *think freely*—has developed within this hard shell, it gradually reacts upon the mentality of the people, who thus gradually become increasingly able to *act freely*. Eventually, it even influences the principle of government, which find that they can themselves profit by treating man, who is *more than a machine*, in a manner appropriate to his dignity. (1991: 59–60)

This possibility, however, eluded Foucault's attention and he attacked the conformity associated with the second recommendation. For Foucault, this recommendation is 'term for term, the opposite of what is ordinarily called freedom of conscience' (1984: 36). He further asks, 'how the use of reason can take the public form that it requires, how the audacity to know can be exercised in broad daylight, while individuals are obeying as scrupulously as possible' (1984: 37).

Foucault is, in an important way, to use Norris's expression, an 'Enlightenment traitor', 'a trenchant critic of Enlightenment'. In my reading, however, there is some scope for ambivalence in Foucault with regard to the Enlightenment, that is, on the question of whether he is pushing further the restricted Kantian plan which would surely mean going beyond Kant. One way of approaching this discussion on Kant and Foucault is to recall and situate both within available paradigms of Classical moral philosophy. This would be despite the fact that the Enlightenment claims to have radically departed from Classical philosophy. (Foucault points out the veracity of this claim, and its limitations.) Broadly speaking, the Kantian position is closer to, or can even be said to inhabit, the Aristotelian paradigm, which allows a discrepancy between moral knowledge and its practice. In contrast, Foucault demands a Socratic adherence to a strict parity between knowing and doing. The Socratic claim does not locate the problem at the domain of practice and the practitioner. This includes both external and internal reasons with regard to the practitioner—internal reasons consist of his or her not seeing the importance of the truth, while an external reason could be a social condition that did not enable the moral agent to practice his or her moral imperative. Through his insistence on the Socratic demand, Foucault forces Kant, and through him the project of Enlightenment, to move from the Aristotelian paradigm to the Socratic paradigm.

The enigma in Foucault's essay is whether it seeks to *complete* the project of Enlightenment by demanding that it should not restrict its act of criticism within the realm of theory but extend it to that of practice. This demand is also the demand made by Socrates. Or does it present the lack of critical apparatus taken beyond thought into action as a defect and denounce the project of Enlightenment? It is not very clear in the essay, which is closer to Foucault. If it is the former, then he cannot be the 'enlightenment traitor' as reckoned by Norris. If it is the latter, then there is the problem of denouncing something merely on the basis of its defects. Pointing out defects need not always be a denouncement. In moral education, the highlighting of defects may be undertaken to improve the situation, to complete the process. This is a serious ambiguity in Foucault's use of his argument in his essay with reference to Kant in particular and the Enlightenment in general.

While Aristotle concedes the possibility of discrepancy between truth and its practice, Socrates equates the two. The interesting thing in the move is that he does not locate the problem of discrepancy within the practice or the practitioner. Rather, he locates the problem within the realm of truth and knowledge of it. If someone does not practice truth, then by definition he or she does not know it. That is, Socrates does not concede the possibility of moral practice outside the domain of knowing truth. Instead, he builds it within that domain. That is, a moral agent not only knows what truth is but this knowledge consists of practicing it. This practice as constituting the knowledge of truth naturally results in such moral agents becoming exemplars. The availability and even the making of these exemplars are an extension or supplement to the moral principles which, as Bilgrami states, are Western moral philosophy's major preoccupation. Thus, in addition to the dispensation of moral principles, we find instances where exemplars too are available in the West. This is in addition to the example of Socrates's life. The moral philosophy of Socrates cannot escape our attention, as it is a dominant strand of philosophical thought in the West. However, Bilgrami's reading of Western moral philosophy does not take into account Socratic thought.

3

EPIC FOR ETHICS

In the previous chapter, we saw that Bilgrami diminished the status of Western moral philosophy by pointing out some of its inherent problems, and then offered Gandhi from India, as an alternative. In contrast, Matilal takes moral discourse in the West as a singular point of reference, and a model for Indian philosophy to emulate. We will examine how Matilal accomplishes this task.

This chapter discusses the problems surrounding Matilal's re-collection and use of the epic, the Mahabharata, and shows how there are many other uses that it is put to. It also explores the nature of representing the epic at the regional level in response to the advent of colonial modernity, by examining its appearance, albeit in disguised form, in a Telugu play, *Kanyasulkam* by Gurajada Apparao. Using a conceptive method, the chapter attempts to cast off this disguise.

It is, or at least appears to be, necessary in modern-day India, to explicate the context of re-reading or recollecting the epics, especially the Mahabharata. The modern Indian re-engagement with the epics may not only reveal a wide spectrum of contemporary needs—intentional, subconscious, or those belonging to collective unconsciousness—but also differences in the social context between two civilizations, modern Western and contemporary Indian. That is, apart from taking into account individual interests and the demands of institutions in the analysis of such re-readings or recollections, there is a need to look deeply into sociological reasons.

There are different levels and means of recollecting or re-reading this epic. In *The Great Indian Novel*, for example, Shashi Tharoor interrogates the Mahabharata as a means of understanding the making of the Indian nation, particularly partition. Matilal's 'Moral Dilemmas of Mahabharata' re-reads, along predictable lines, this classical text from India, against the backdrop of modern Western philosophy. These two trajectories illustrate two vital contemporary uses the epic is put to, namely, the national and the international.[1] There is yet another level at which the epic is made to function, that is, at the regional level. And engaging with the regional, at least in India, is an essential ingredient in determining the nature of the Indian nation. Regional languages provide an important element of cultural federalism to India. It is another matter that swayed by politics, this cultural federalism has not been taken seriously. The importance of the region in India cannot be ignored.

Departing from the present obsession with the derivative character of Indian nationalism *a la* Partha Chatterjee, while acknowledging the insights this provides, I would like to engage with the question of what the Indian nation derives from by scrutinizing the constituents of the Indian nation. The West, from which we may say the Indian nation is derived, consists of autonomous individuals and citizens, and, it has necessarily had to exit from pre-modern realities. Ernest Renon brilliantly captures this idea when he writes—'To forget and—I will venture to say—to get one's history wrong are essential factors in the making of the nation' (1939: 190). This historical amnesia provides the requisite raw material to produce the space, an almost empty social space, the *tabula rasa* of John Locke, or man-in-the-state-of-nature in Social Contract philosophers, where new, autonomous individuals are made to stand to form the nation. In contrast, the constituents of the Indian nation are family, region, *bhasha*, the past, and so on. Hence, to understand the nation in India, unlike a nation in the West, it is necessary to acknowledge its contents. In sum, focusing on the constituents of the Indian nation would reveal the non-derivative aspects of Indian nationalism.

That is, in addition to the two trajectories described which the epic is made to traverse, namely, the national and the international, I will add another function for the epic and, a particularly interesting one, that is, its use in the regional domain. This is my first claim in this chapter.[2]

Let me locate my discussion of Matilal's engagement with the epic more clearly within the broader issues under consideration—in the context of discussing the nature of moral dilemmas in this epic, Matilal claims that 'some of these moral dilemmas ... are illustrations of perennial problems in moral philosophy'. Discerning the difference between the practical and moral realms, he declares that some of these dilemmas have 'no satisfactory solution, although, in each one, an *ad hoc* practical action-guide was devised in the original story while the main problem remained unsolved' (2002: 21). His next point is of immense interest. He states—'Over the ages we notice that various episodes and subplots of these epic stories have been retold with great ingenuity in various regional and vernacular versions of the epics, in folk-tales, plays, dramas, etc. Each new version may be regarded as a novel attempt to resolve the dilemma inherent in the original version' (2002: 21).

In order to bolster my argument let me identify three aspects of this statement by Matilal. In addition to his own use of the epic he registers another, existing use of the epic, namely, its continuous and ingenuous retelling in regional and vernacular versions. This to me is a great point. However, Matilal does not pursue it. Having made the point, he goes on to do something like this—In the very next section he begins by endorsing the view of V. S. Sukthankar expressed in 1942 that 'Indians still stand under the spell of the *Mahābhārata* ... [and it is] a "dateless and deathless poem ... which forms the strongest link between India old and new"' (2002: 21). Matilal then establishes a philosophical path wherein he relates the epic with the realm of ethics. To elaborate—he identifies an absence by stating that with the exception of, 'some cursory comments and some insightful observations, the professional philosophers in India have very seldom discussed what we call moral philosophy today'

(2002: 22). Matilal proceeds to fill this absence with the moral dilemmas in the Mahabharata. He writes, 'The moral dilemmas presented in the *Mahābhārata* are in some sense universal, for most of them can be effectively used even today to illustrate arguments in moral philosophy' (2002: 23). This project takes him to engage with Donald Davidson's view of 'weakness of will as incontinence', with Kant, R. M. Hare, Sartre, and so on. At the end of the essay, Matilal discusses the debate between Bankim and Tagore on this issue, and concludes, 'All this shows how concerned our present-day moral thinking still is with the dilemmas presented in the traditional epics' (2002: 35). Thus, we may say that Matilal spends the resources of the epic to get ethics in Indian thought.

First, the move to put the epic to a merely ethical use is a problematic one; the epic has a larger task. It is necessary to explore a more complex relationship between the epic and ethics. While Matilal may not deny such a relationship, the problem with his philosophical project is that in his preoccupation or mere obsession with modern Western philosophy he does not make use of this complex relationship between epic and ethics.

Second, while admitting the limitations attending the continuity between past and present, one may discuss the epic's involvement in the bhasha realm in modes that are not continuous. I want to examine this involvement while keeping in mind the complex changes taking place in contemporary Indian society. That is, I want to explore how this recalling of the epic is necessitated by the sociological requirement.

Third, I want to examine the vernacular and regional uses that Matilal refers to but does not engage with. Further, my engagement with the epic in the vernacular will not pursue a trajectory along the lines of its ingenuous 'retelling' or be directed towards seeing pervasive continuity between the past and the present. I want to claim more than ingenuity and novelty.

As a preface to my argument, let me point out that the relationship between the pre-modern/traditional and the modern in the West is sequential in nature. There is first the pre-modern *then* the modern. More importantly, entry into the modern requires pass of clearance certificate at the gate that the pre-modern is disinherited. In other words, the new, atomized individuals do not occupy already available spaces left over from the pre-modern. As stated before, those from the past need to clearly and wholly exit from it to self-start, as it were, the new modern.

While modernity travelled to India via colonialism, the success of its penetration into India is viewed differently by different commentators. There are those, like Daya Krishna, who allege that colonialism killed Indian philosophy, a statement which plainly concedes the success of colonialism. Krishna pictured Indian philosophy as 'dead and mummified' (1996: 15). In contrast, those like Sri Aurobindo maintained that the effect of the entry of colonialism into India resulted merely in a surface deterioration; the core remained intact. He insisted that 'the Indian brain is still in potentiality what it was; but it is being damaged, stunted and defaced. The greatness of its innate possibilities is hidden by the greatness of its surface deterioration' ('The Brain of India', Volume 3, 1972: 339).

While these two diametrically opposite views can provide enough intellectual resources for a debate, as in all debates the truth might be found in between the two, a space which is generally more accessible to viewers of the debate than to the contestants. A version of this in-between space that I want to explore here is the idea that the relationship between the pre-modern and the modern in India seems to be simultaneous. Both modern and pre-modern seem to co-exist in various forms and relations in India. To be more specific, while at the global and national levels India seems to have a modern form, the contents of this form seem to be predominantly drawn from the pre-modern. While we need modern vocabulary and systems of thought to understand the form, we also need the texts from the past to make sense of the pre-modern social realities that constitute the contents. This is one of the substantial reasons for recalling the epic.

It is this sociological requirement rather than the normative need that underlies the contemporary re-invocation of the epic. This is what distinguishes those Indian scholars who recollected or re-read their pasts, from recollections or re-reading of the past by Western scholars such as Leo Strauss and Alasdair MacIntyre. The latter scholars' recollections are inevitably stuck in the romantic problematic. They recall texts from the past only when past realities have been disinherited and dismantled (for more on this see my 2011). In contrast, one may put forward the example of Amartya Sen, who claims that the perpetuation of secularism and democracy in India depends upon the argumentativeness of Indians.[3] The implication of this discrepancy between the impact of modernity in the West and in India is interesting. With the exit of the pre-modern, modernity as a secondary obligation, or a token of its magnanimity, conceded a psychological requirement. That is, it allowed the reclamation of what had been lost in reality, within the imagination. Art, literature, libraries, museums, and galleries came to fulfil this requirement. Remnants from the pre-modern are transformed into synthetic sensibilities, quarantined so that they do not become true realities, and remain largely within the realm of imagination. They have very little sociological status and are barely endowed with political consequences. Hence, there is a need to identify the politics of these disciplines like art and literature. The epics, along with other pre-modern forms, inhabit this imaginary realm. This becomes clear when one closely examines the use of the epic in the West.

In contrast, given the sociological fact of the pre-modern co-existing with the modern in India, epics and literary works have not only a romantic role to play, but, in addition, can and do discharge a sociological role, and threaten to have political implications. In fact, I have argued elsewhere (2011), against the proposal to privilege social theory over literary domains, that there is more descriptive content and insight within the literary domain in India than has been revealed by social theory. In this context, I gave the example of how Krishna Sobti's *Sikka Badal Gaya* is more insightful in describing communalism in India than several thousand scholarly papers written on this topic. Thus, I find the literary domain to be a more fertile terrain to explore contemporary India than social theory. So, while the artistic and literary domains in the West, subsequent to modernity, were creatively quarantined, in India they continue to enjoy a sociological

status and discharge political duties. Here I will discuss one important
role they play in India.

Literature in India, despite the tremendous impact of English literature, largely retained its region-specific elements. Let us understand
the complexity surrounding this, that is, receiving influences from
outside, yet retaining regional specificity, with an illustration from the
author of the work that I am going to discuss here, namely, Gurajada
Apparao who wrote *Kanyasulkam*. Apparao began writing poetry
in English during his school days and subsequently gave this up to
start writing in Telugu.[4] The contributing factor behind this move
needs to be explicated. Was it his inability to write in English, and
compete against native speakers of the language, or was it dictated by
necessities imposed by his native context? For instance, his decision
may have been affected by the need to communicate to his audience,
or by a desire for social reform. Post-colonial writers like Gayatri
Spivak have been criticized by theorists such as Terry Eagleton for
the fact that the post-colonial subjects about whom they write do not
understand their writings. So, the fruit of the decision to write in their
own mother tongue or native languages leave bhashas in India as a
strong presence. I will explore below a text from one of the regional
bhashas, namely, Telugu, in the context of our discussion on the epic
Mahabharata.

Telugu Text and the Epic: Kanyasulkam *and* the Mahabharata

There is a close and complex relationship between *Kanyasulkam*
and the Mahabharata, yet this has eluded the attention of scholars so
far. I will now discuss how this has happened and what is responsible
for this. As a background to this, let me discuss the play.

As pointed out by the well-known writer Arudra, *Kanyasulkam*,
by Gurajada Apparao, is the first play to have as its two primary
axes, 'spoken Telugu' and 'social reform' (1985: iii).[5] This makes it
the foundational text of modern Telugu. The play was written and

first staged in 1892, and published in 1897. The second edition of the play, which is significantly different from the first one, was published in 1909. There is a lot of controversy with regard to the difference between the two versions. Some see it as an original and an improved version, whereas others understand them as two radically different works. The reasons for the difference between the two versions have been widely discussed. Velcheru Narayana Rao (hereafter V. N. Rao) holds that the writer's relationship with the Maharaja of Vijayanagaram was responsible for this difference. I shall come to this later. *Kanyasulkam* continues to be the most successful and popular play. The text ran into several editions, yielded many performances, and was even made into a film with N. T. Rama Rao and Savitri in the cast.[6]

To partially paraphrase V. N. Rao's summary of the play, it is about a social evil, namely, the giving of girl children in marriage to very old men in exchange for money. Lubdha Avadhanlu, an old Brahmin, arranges to marry the young daughter of another Brahmin, Agni Hotra Avadhanlu. Both men have daughters who are already widows. Greed and fear of wrath or impending misfortune are the factors that drive them towards arranging this marriage. The bride's mother in this case, however, is against the marriage. She threatens to commit suicide if the marriage is held, as her other daughter, Buccamma, is already a widow. Her brother, Karataka Sastri, comes to her rescue. He promises her that he will stop the marriage. He disguises his disciple as a girl and himself as a *Gunturu Sastrulu* (a Sastri from the town in coastal Andhra Pradesh called Guntur), and travels to Lubdh Avadhanlu's village. He takes the help of a 'pleasure-woman' (I am using V. N. Rao's translation of original Telugu terms), Madhura Vani, who traps her paramour Ramap Pantulu into cancelling the previous arrangement and offering the unsuspecting Lubdha Avadhanlu's marriage to the disguised young boy disciple instead, for a lower price. After the marriage takes place the bride disappears, and the bridegroom is charged with murder. Saujanya Rao defends Lubdha Avadhanlu's case but finds it difficult as there is no evidence. At this juncture Madhura Vani, disguised as a man, comes to Saujanya Rao's house and offers to help him with evidence in exchange for a kiss. This is an important move because Saujanya Rao is known to be wise, pious, and honest. He is against prostitution. In the end he falls for Madhura Vani and agrees to kiss her, but she stops him saying that she has promised her mother that she will not defile the innocent, thereby exposing his moral weakness and upholding her own virtues.

There is a parallel story, of Girisam, who visits Agni Hotra Avadhanlu's house on the pretext of tutoring the latter's son Venkatesam during vacation. There he falls in love with Agni Hotra Avadhanlu's widowed but beautiful daughter Buccamma. He had previously cohabited with a widow, and then with Madhura Vani. Madhura Vani meets Girisam in Saujanya Rao's house and reveals his past at Saujanya Rao's request.

Several aspects of the play are of interest. For example, it does not have a hero. Every character has a limitation or weakness. The play is an instance of the distribution or decentralization of human weakness. There is no heroic figure, no idea, ideal, or era which is represented as worthy of eulogizing. The shortcomings and weaknesses of both individuals and institutions are highlighted, including Brahmanism, colonialism, and cultural traditions. At the same time, there is no anti-hero, or *khalnayak*.

In addition to this, if one observes the play carefully, there is an attempt to hold up and compare the practices of the higher caste, particularly the Brahmins, and those like Madhura Vani who is a 'pleasure-woman'. For instance, when Karataka Sastri tells his disciple, while holding a Sanskrit text, 'Here, I take the oath holding this book', the disciple replies, 'No, I don't believe in Sanskrit books anymore. We need something weighty. Should I go get an English book from Girisam-garu?' (2011: 41).[7] Later, Ramap Pantulu discloses—'I bribed Siddhanti to read Lubdha's horoscope. He looked at it from top to bottom and said he saw a marriage very soon and a lot of money from it too. Since then the old man has been pulled both ways' (2011: 56).

At another time he says—'No, this time it's not my doing. Agni-[H]
otra Avadhanlu fixed the horoscope himself. This is common among
us Brahmins. Not one horoscope we show for matchmaking is true;
every one of them is fixed' (2011: 56).

While these episodes and the plot as a whole question and cast
doubts upon the morals and stature of the higher caste Brahmin
characters, there is a simultaneous effort towards ennobling and
raising the status of the 'pleasure-woman', Madhura Vani. However,
interestingly, she herself makes no attempt to justify either her
profession or individuals who share her profession. She only claims
that she is different. She says, 'Just because I'm a pleasure-woman,
you can't take me lightly. Even *we* have our morals' (2011: 16). She
says—

> I wouldn't have accepted your two hundred [rupees] if I had known
> that your lands are mortgaged to your debtors. You should cut down
> on your expenditure, begin saving, pay off your debts, and put your
> house in order. I get a good name only if people say that Pantulu-garu
> so-and-so kept such-and-such a pleasure-woman and flourished from
> her love and care. This is my family tradition, Pantulu-garu! I am not
> like all other pleasure-women in town. (2011: 54)

Further, she says to Karataka Sastri who is in disguise as Gunturu
Sastrulu—'By profession I am a pleasure-woman. I take money for
my services whenever I can. But did you think Madhuravani has no
kindness or compassion? Do I expect money to save your sister?'
(2011: 65).

The next point of interest is that the most pervasive feature of
the play is satire. It is through satire that the social evil, which is
the subject of the play, is explicated. The use of satire to expose the
truth here is akin to Charlie Chaplin's use of satire in his films. The
absence of heroism, and satire, are two important structural aspects
of the play. The third important aspect of the play is its time and
context. Before I discuss the third point, I will briefly discuss two
diametrically opposite interpretations of this text. V. N. Rao, an emi-
nent critic and translator, was in favour of the second interpretation.

Crisply summarizing the first interpretation while placing the play in context, V. N. Rao writes—

> Critics who have written about this play in Telugu have consistently maintained that it was written in strong support of social reform against a number of social evils, including the tradition of selling girls as brides, the custom which prohibited widow remarriage, and the prevalence of 'nautch girls' (i.e., women who gave sexual service to men in return for money), and hailed Apparao as the harbinger of a cultural renaissance in Telugu following Bengali social reformers. (2011: xvii)

Gurajada Apparao has been eulogized as *yugakarta*, *shakapurushudu* by critics like Arudra. Hence, his play may be seen as a progressive work that is seeking to eliminate social evil and revolutionize the society. Both liberals and the radicals held this view and rallied around this text, projecting Apparao as a modern radical. Sri Sri, another revolutionary poet and writer, went to the extent of declaring *Gurujadadiadugujada* (We follow the footsteps of Gurajada). He recommended readers to—

> Follow his footsteps, they are the way to the future.
> Gurajada cures us of stupidity in our nature.
> (Quoted from V. N. Rao's translation in 2011: 284)

Later, however, Sri Sri denied this and called himself the *Vaitalika* of modern Telugu. In any case, the point remains that *Kanyasulkam* has been historically projected as a revolutionary text and hailed as the foundational text of modern Telugu literature.

In contradistinction to this widely accepted interpretation, V. N. Rao insisted that 'Apparao's play is a continuation of the literary traditions deriving from ... pre-colonial modernity' and shows how the new middle class 'accepted the representation of Indian society as stagnant and decadent and of Indians as a group of people steeped in superstition and immorality, insensitive to human values and incapable of changing' (2011: 249). The acceptance of such a representation by the middle class was, in V. N. Rao's view, largely due to the influence of colonial modernity in the early nineteenth century. In contrast to this amnesia about themselves as continuations of literary traditions deriving from 'pre-colonial modernity' amongst the new middle class, V. N. Rao wrote, 'we come across the characters in Apparao's play'. They are 'dynamic, enterprising, creative, funny, intriguing, tough, and they seem to be having good time besides' (2011: 249). V. N. Rao goes further to claim that 'Apparao is not presenting a society that is deteriorating, nor is it in any moral crisis. And if there is an occasional violation of the moral order, the play strongly suggests that this society itself is capable of setting it right with a strong sense of purpose and determination' (2011: 249).

Thus, he concludes—

Clearly this is not a society in need of social reform. Apparao also suggests, equally strongly, that the impact of colonialism is debilitating even for a confident society such as this one and that the society's upper castes are losing their fundamental character under the corrupting influence of colonial administration. In this, Apparao is an extraordinarily original writer with an understanding of social reality, very different from many writers of his time, including the more celebrated Bankim and Tagore. (2011: 249–50)

The first interpretation makes some exaggerated claims, while the second contains a grain of truth. On the other hand, there is an element of truth in the first interpretation and excessive complacency in the second. Both interpretations are partially accurate as the evidence they selectively cite in support of their arguments largely upholds those arguments rigorously and consistently. One can see exactly what each is trying to show from the perspective they identify.

However, the problem with the first interpretation is that the pervasive presence of the social evil portrayed requires that if the play be politically viable, there needs to be a hero, or an era to emulate. There is no character in the play which is cast as an absolute hero. Each one has human follies. And no one, including Saujanya Rao, seems to be worth emulating. So the absence of a hero, rather than the presence of an anti-hero, causes it to lack any political solution. In other words, no alternative utopia, either in India's past or in colonial modernity, is suggested in the play. British, especially that of modernity as alternatives are not clearly endorsed or considered by Apparao. Moreover, the police, the judiciary, and even the English education practiced by local Indians, are portrayed as essentially farcical. Therefore, this interpretation suffers from excess. Yet, it is not a tragedy or an absurd play. So, if everyone in the play makes mistakes, whom do we look to, to provide for emulation? There is as yet no possibility of a solution to social evils such as the practice of kanyasulkam. This can be seen as an excellent example of Foucault's thesis of the pervasiveness of power without ways out. This, then, is the serious problem at the heart of this interpretation, for which there is no satisfactory answer.

The problem with the second interpretation is that it portrays Andhra society and culture during the period as too complacent or internally self-sufficient to effect the changes required. Here, V. N. Rao presents a succinct but brilliant statement as evidence in support of his claim—'Let us take a look at the central event of the play—the wedding of a child to an old man—the supposed evil that social reformers were making a song and dance about. As soon as such a wedding is announced, a whole village, across all castes, unites to prevent it from happening' (2011: 272).

From this, he rightly and crisply concludes—'This clearly is not a society that normally allows such marriage to take place. They [themselves] have come to know that the practice is wrong. Why would anyone make a big issue of reforming such a society unless they were rather simple-minded and naive like Saujanya Rao ...' (2011: 272–3).

This is the strong point of V. N. Rao's argument, namely, that the problem is recognized by the insiders. One might also agree with his claim that the author of the play is in favour of 'change', not the version of change drawn from colonial modernity, but taken instead from pre-colonial modernity in India, which is defined as existing from the 'late fifteenth to the eighteenth centuries' (2011: 247). Yet what seems to go against this interpretation is the absence of remedy or solution to the problem in the play. This goes against V. N. Rao's claim that what is portrayed is a confident society and not a deteriorating one. Further, V. N. Rao claims that the author of the play does not want to protect 'Indian civilization from the influence of Western culture' (2011: 290). He seeks to disconnect the influence of Western modernity from the play and to connect it instead to pre-colonial Indian modernity. He, however, does not clarify how the author of the play, who, he says, does not protect Indian civilization from the influence of Western culture, can receive Western culture. So, this second interpretation suffers from lack, that is, the opposite of excess. V. N. Rao's interpretation is problematic because having retrieved the text from the social reformists who he claims are the products of colonial modernity, he, instead of restoring to it an autonomous status, pushes it into the other side of the ethical, rendering it vulnerable in a different way.

This is one set of disagreements that I have with these two versions. They largely relate to assumptions about their views. My further disagreement with the existing interpretations of this text is with regard to the realm in which they belong, namely, the ethical realm. The important thing to note here is that these two diametrically opposite versions are at the level of the political or ethical realm. Here I would like to introduce how the ethical realm, without the epical realm, can conceal some important structural aspects, crucial to the text. To lay this bare it is necessary to return to the point I made a little while ago. One of the structural features of this text is that there is no character in the play that is above folly, particularly human folly. In this I make a distinction between human folly and folly due to divine dispensation. Everyone in the play has human weaknesses. More importantly and in contrast to this, a 'pleasure-woman' like Madhura Vani is endowed with some virtues. Hence, this is either a case of distributive evil or folly, or there is an attempt in this play to decentralize and democratize evil thereby making it more prone to reform than revolution, or sticking with the status quo. The question that I want to probe further is whether the recognition of this feature in the play makes me leave the ethical realm and, while exploring outside the ethical space, whether I locate the play's proximity to the epic, Mahabharata.

Some parts of the pre-modern in the West were historically quarantined; however, I will argue in the next chapter that some texts belonging to the pre-modern in India have, as one may say, gone on sabbatical, in reaction to modernity. I now want to propose a hypothesis, that with the advent of modernity in India some pre-modern texts have disguised[8] themselves and withdrawn into the bhashas. I have exposed one of them elsewhere, showing how the famous radical feminist novel in Telugu by Gudipati Venkata Chalam is in fact the Telugu *prabandham*, *Tarasashankam* (2003). I now want to propose that *Kanyasulkam* is the Mahabharata in disguise.

My first argument in support of this is that just as in the Mahabharata, in *Kanyasulkam* no one is above folly. Everyone has human weaknesses and makes mistakes. So unlike the Ramayana which has a clearly identified hero in Rama, the Mahabharata is more distributive and decentralized in narrating the human condition and its predicament. My second reason for advancing this view is that close scrutiny reveals resemblances between Girisam and Krishna, Madhura Vani and Draupadi, Saujanya Rao and Dharma Raja.

Finally, there are three important disguises in *Kanyasulkam*. That of Karataka Sastri as Guntur Sastrulu, his disciple as a bride, and Madhura Vani disguised as a male entering Saujanya Rao's house. Critics, including the ingenious V. N. Rao, have not paid enough attention to the very important element of disguise. My contention is that disguise may be immoral but it requires more cognitive competence than merely telling the truth (for more on this, see Akeel Bilgrami 2006). Just as Dharma Raja (Yudhishthir), who stands for truth, does not tell a lie or is not perhaps competent to tell a lie, Saujanya Rao can only be moral, and he is not capable of disguising himself. Disguise is important because it is at the very core of the play. It is instrumental in bringing about the play's climax and achieving the desired effect on the audience. It is therefore necessary to recognize its importance in order to understand the nature of the sub-text in the play. Thus, in similar vein to the importance of the disguises in the play, I want to argue that the epic has disguised itself within the play in response to the advent of modernity.

My fourth reason for proposing that the *Kanyasulkam* is in fact the Mahabharata, is the detailed discussion at the end of the play about the Bhagavad Gita, which is considered by many to be a part of the Mahabharata. Madhura Vani, arguing with Saujanya Rao while in disguise, tells him that her mother taught her 'to be good to good people and bad to bad people'. He responds, 'Your mother has to be respected. I suggest you follow the first half of her teaching and try to change the second half. Be good to bad people too'. Then he continues, 'Also who is good and who is bad? There is always some good in bad things and bad in good things' (2011: 230). Pursuing the debate, Madhura Vani, still in disguise, asks Saujanya Rao, who is strongly against prostitution, that while it is true that 'Pleasure women may be bad as a caste. But, sir, as you yourself have said, isn't there some good in everything bad?' (2011: 234). She subsequently removes her disguise. Saujanya Rao is astonished and calls her act 'treachery'. She replies by drawing his attention to the maxim— 'A teacher should not forget his own teaching, sir' (2011: 237). An important aspect of this discussion is the equal distribution of good and evil without allowing either to be concentrated in one place or consolidated exclusively and separately. Such a feature does not allow any hero or heroic element to flourish in the play.

After the argument described earlier, Madhura Vani finds a book in Saujanya Rao's room which turns out to be the Bhagavad Gita. He tells her that this 'is a book that converts bad people into good people [and those] who read it find an invaluable friend', that is, he means Lord Krishna (2011: 241). Madhura Vani asks him whether Krishna would make friends with a *nautch*-girl or pleasure-woman to which he replies yes, Krishna would 'make friends with anyone who believes in him'. She then reveals her verbal trap by asking, 'So, Krishna is not *anti-nautch*?' (2011: 241). It is particularly interesting that this concluding part of the play contains a discussion on the Gita and Krishna when the more appropriate text would be the Ramayana.

To posit further similarities between *Kanyasulkam* and the Mahabharata, the earlier discussion is of substantial interest because Saujanya Rao stands for dharma, and he is against *adharma*. His personality is trapped in the groove of dharma. Yet the text, Bhagavad Gita, which he vouches for, has a different and more complex relation between dharma and adharma. For instance, in this text, there is no attempt either to eliminate or even to maintain distance towards adharma. Therefore, some features of the epic do appear in the play. This is another point in support of my argument about the disguise of the Mahabharata.

Yet another similarity between the two, that underlines the disguised nature of the epic, is the presence of a metanarrative, which disturbs our reception of the narrative and internally subverts the story, in both the Mahabharata and *Kanyasulkam*. At the end of the Mahabharata, the narrator announces his intervention by throwing up his hands and complains that nobody listens to him. A parallel appears in the final passage of the play, where Girisam interjects, '*Damn it*, the story has taken a wrong turn' (2011: 244).

Finally, let me add that V. N. Rao in his critical interpretation of the play comes very close to recognizing the similarities between the Telugu play and the epic—

Indian readers are not unacquainted with polyphonic works. The epics, the Mahābhārata and the Rāmāyana, are dialogical and polyphonic. Their polyphony is what allows numerous retellings with points of view that extend, deviate, contest, and contradict the meaning 'intended' by the legendary 'authors' Vyāsa and Vālmīki. Indian literature has hundreds of such retellings in every language, including Sanskrit. But even if the readers had perceived the polyphony in the great epics, they probably would not notice it in Apparao, for they could not imagine that Apparao, a mere mortal, might belong to the same class as the ancient greats. Furthermore, dominant practices of interpretation of the play, which I will explain later, foreclosed all possibilities of the reader seeing polyphony in Apparao's work. (2011: 261–2)

In my reading, this comparison between the epics by V. N. Rao is not incidental. I think a closer reading of the play, at least indirectly, forced him, perhaps unconsciously, to recall the epics. V. N. Rao claims that the play and the epics have polyphony as a common structural feature, thereby establishing a common ground. Having established this illuminating comparison he writes that readers of the play were unable to recognize the polyphony in it. It is this, according to him that prevents them from conceding to Apparao the status of the epic writers. This speculation, which is not elaborated, remains incomplete as it hides from V. N. Rao crucial commonalities between the play and the epic.

The other important point in the passage from V. N. Rao is in the recognition of the polyphonic nature of the epics, acknowledging the extent of its numerous retellings as consisting of only, deviation, contestation, contradicting the intended meaning of the author. I want to argue for the inclusion of disguise as another important feature of polyphony. Readers may have reservations about comparing Apparao with the ancient greats, but if he is considered to be the author disguising the epic then they may attribute more ingenuity and creativity to him.

Unlike the existing uses of the epic that are more causal in nature, I want to consider a close yet non-causal relation that contains in itself an imperative need to disguise the original. The need to go in disguise was required by the necessity imposed by the context, namely, the advent of modernity. More importantly, V. N. Rao's discussion on the polyphony of the epic does bring him to the question of the epic nature in the play. However, he shies away from it, largely due to his preoccupation with refuting the dominant interpretation of the play.

Thus, I want to argue in support of my hypothesis that, with the advent of modernity, unlike in the West where they have been quarantined, in India texts belonging to the pre-modern have, some of them, gone on sabbatical, some in disguise. Therefore we must ask ourselves, what is our role today as critics in regard to these texts? What are the politics behind disclosing the texts in disguise? Are we not committing a breach of trust by revealing their real identity? Yes, in a way we are. But I would like to look at this quite differently. I want to argue that the texts that are in disguise because of the presence of colonialism have forgotten that they are in disguise and their purpose. Now it is time for them to remember their hidden natures, shed the disguises, and reveal their real characters. I think it is the responsibility of critics to lay bare this literary genealogy. The critic now has to enter into the green room and start removing the make-up, thus restoring the original. This is an enormous task and can form a new agenda for the rejuvenation of epics in the changed scenario of contemporary India. What we have in front of us is unprecedented and extremely challenging. It would also reveal an ingenuous way of responding to the threats by modernity. For instance, one way of responding is by retreating into the suburbs, thereby changing the relation between the centre-periphery. Modernity threatens the native and the native is defeated. When modernity threatened the pre-modern West, certain things that are destroyed in reality are reclaimed in art and literature and are quarantined (that is, museums and art galleries). This is also what has happened in India; we have mimicked these actions of the West too. There is a third way that is prevalent in India, namely, the pre-modern texts have gone on sabbatical, or are in disguise. We need different kinds of mechanisms to understand this process—we need to deal with them—engage with the bhashas—treat them as reality; this is even if we reject some of it later. I do not want to place the moral realm before the factual realm. We have to move away from the centre, whether in terms of the epic or modernity, and address the bhashas which are in the margins. Here, I want to concede more strength to colonial modernity than V. N. Rao does and then work towards discovering the ways in which it was and is combated. This is also an opportunity to claim that the impact of colonial modernity has been positively used to enrich the suburb, which in the literary domain stands for the bhashas which represent the cultural federalism of India.

The route between the epic and the regional—or the bhashas—which is merely mentioned by Matilal but not discussed in detail, is of immense importance in understanding the epics, and not merely in order to put them to national or international uses. On closer scrutiny, one can find an ascending order in the use of the epic. Matilal's negotiation for the use of the epic at the international level is an explicit one. Its use as a novel and at the national level by Tharoor is less explicit. The use of the epic at the bhasha level, in disguise, is still less explicit. My intention is to elucidate the range and extent of the creative uses of the epic, from the international domain to the national, and further to the regional, and to clarify the creative possibilities the epic offers. Hence, in addition to getting an ethics for India which, in Matilal's reckoning Indian philosophy lacks, there are other important and spirited tasks the Indian epic has performed.

In the first part of this book, Chapters One and Two discussed problems relating to the offering of Indian solutions for Western problems. I have argued that there are internal resources in the predecessors to Kant and moral philosophy, in the form of Christianity, Christ, and Socrates which obviate the requirement for Indian solutions. Chapter 3 shows how internal resources in India can be put not only to international uses but may address urgent needs in the domain of the region. The present chapter may be seen as offering not mere alternatives to the West but the means of using internal resources, for instance, combating colonialism by escaping into the territory of the regional. This is an essential move because the region is a difficult and rough terrain which the outsider finds difficult to encroach upon or penetrate, though in varying degrees. The next part analyses how contemporary Indian philosophers, in their preoccupation with their ancestors, have neglected their predecessors. It explicates the problems surrounding both their obsessions and their neglect.

Notes

1. Following counter-factual logic, what would have happened to this use if the epic was not available? Whether alternative resources would have been pressed into service or affecting this use would not have arisen in the first place.

2. There is some difference in the recent interests, particularly amongst the academic institutions, to rally around this text. Limitations in the vocabulary of secular rhetoric are one of the reasons to turn towards those texts that are non-secular though not necessarily anti-secular. While accepting the truth in this line of argument I would want to transcend this negative feeling and embark on a more positive domain. There are those who participated in this recalling in a romantic and almost self-forgetting mode, eulogizing the golden periods of the past. This in one sense did not take seriously the important presences, interventions, and mediations from the outside.

3. He claims that the 'richness of the tradition of argument make much difference' in 'great many different ways' to 'subcontinental lives today'. It contributes in shaping India's 'social world and the nature' of its culture, in making 'heterodoxy the natural state of affairs in India'. Arguments are an important part of our public life and this 'deeply influences Indian politics, and is particularly relevant, I would argue, to the development of democracy in India and emergence of its secular priorities' (2005: 12). Reinforcing this he goes on to assert that even though 'Indian democracy remains imperfect and flawed in several different ways ... the ways and means of overcoming these faults can draw powerfully on the argumentational tradition' (2005: 13).

4. Sudhir Chandra informed me that this is a transnational feature, as Bankim, Michael Madhusudhan Dutt, R. C. Dutt, and many others toed the same trajectory.

5. The problem with associating social reform with *Kanyasulkam* is that it assumes that Indian society has a centre which needs to be reformed. The interesting aspect of this play is to show that Indian society has no such centre; hence to reform it is not going to be a major success. However, this society has several centres with a shifting hierarchy. So the very nature of the text such as *Kanyasulkam*, which I claim is derived from the epic Mahabharata, is polyphonic, and not merely the reading of this text, as it is sometimes claimed on behalf of them. It is this lack of single centredness, the absence of *a* hero that is common to both these texts.

6. There are several Tollywood versions of the contemporary use of the epic, notable one is Bapu's *Manavooripandavulu*. Bapu who is ardent devotee of Rama and Ramayana deviated and made this film with Mahabharata as a background. And there is Bollywood—*Kalyug* by Shyam Benegal and several others.

7. All quotations from this play are from Velcheru Narayana Rao's translation into English under the title, *Girls for Sale: A Play from Colonial India*.

8. Ashis Nandy in his *Intimate Enemy* refers to the dehumanized self. While
agreeing with him, I want to add that the oppressed also have deployed
disguise to escape the cultural onslaught of colonialism and modernity
(1994).

II

Ancestors and Predecessors

4

THE TEXTS ON SABBATICAL

There is a story of Kumbhakarna in the epic Ramayana. He sleeps uninterruptedly for six months in a year. He is endowed with a boon that ensures he cannot be defeated while he is awake, but if woken from sleep his winning is not guaranteed. He is killed because he is woken up from sleep to fight in the war with Sri Rama.

There are two important limitations, which are structural in nature, which seem to have caused at least one of the projects of Daya Krishna for Indian philosophy—*Samvāda*—to incite despair in him and others who toed his line. I make a distinction between the project that he initiated and the path that he actually followed. While accepting the significance of the former I will point out the limitations of the latter. First, let me recall some of the salient features of the project. One of the major projects of Daya Krishna, in my reading, is to account for classical presences that are absent in the contemporary. It was this preoccupation with the metaphysics of absence that led him to this project which he undertook along with others. They include M. P. Rege, R. C. Dwivedi, Mukund Lath, some Sanskritists, and modern scholars of philosophy. This project initiated a dialogue between modern logicians and traditional pandits. This project, it may be pointed out, inhabited the contemporary philosophical terrain initiated by B. K. Matilal. This terrain creates temporal imbalance in which contemporary Western philosophy is compared or contrasted with classical Indian philosophy. I have discussed the nature and implications of this limitation in detail in my book (Raghuramaraju 2006). In the present chapter, I will discuss yet another structural limitation constraining the *Samvāda* project.

Let me begin with a simple distinction, that between author and reader; between the author's intention and the reader's perception; what is created and how it is received. In the history of human thought, there are some significant instances where what is thought to be a profound text is not received as such, and there are instances where what is not so profound is received very well, and there are also interesting instances where what the author considers to be an important work is not received as such, but his or her less significant work is hailed as outstanding. For instance, it is said that Adam Smith considered his work on moral philosophy to be more significant than his work on political economy for which he was acclaimed. There are other instances where something that has been received in a limited sense in one form comes to have extended importance in other forms. This is the case with the novel *Devdas* by Sarat Chandra and the films based on the novel. From this we can infer that there is a domain outside the purview of the text and the author. One aspect of this limited purview is discussed intensively in reader studies. Here, I want to bring into the discussion another aspect of this extended domain, namely, the mood of the time. Amongst several available texts some texts are received more enthusiastically than others despite being dismissed as insignificant in influential opinion. Similarly, some texts might not be well received despite being promoted by influential opinion. There is a host of reasons that contribute to these developments. In the following pages I will discuss an instance of certain old classical texts which were recalled, yet the context of their resuscitation did not enable the desired results. I will identify the social factors that failed to facilitate these results.

Daya Krishna and others have initiated *Samvāda* to instill new life into contemporary Indian philosophy. One of its major aims is to foster dialogue between modern logicians and traditional Indian pandits. Other aims include engagement with Kashmiri Saivism, Bhakti, *Vastusastra*, and Arabic and Persian traditions. In this chapter, I will confine my discussion to the major attempt at a 'first record of a dialogue between philosophers trained in the classical Indian tradition of philosophizing and those trained in the contemporary western tradition on a philosophical theme which is both contemporary, and primarily western' (Krishna et al. 1991: xi). This, they believed, would set in motion both creative and productive elements in Indian philosophy. Stating the purpose and goals of the *Samvāda* project, Rege wrote that—'Indian philosophy, though not stagnant, has developed much more slowly and over a narrow area as it remained wedded to traditional forms of knowledge .... The only way to revitalize it is to bring it in to the arena of modern, i.e., western thought' (Ibid.: xxiv). Therefore, the project envisaged that dialogue between Sanskrit pandits and modern Western logicians would revitalize philosophical activity which had been progressing slowly and within narrow domains. By establishing a dialogue with modern Western logic scholars, the speed of progress, it was thought, would increase, and a greater openness achieved. This project is not only desirable, ambitious, and creative but has also been clearly planned through serious deliberation. It has the advantage of having the experience of senior Indian philosophers.

It is important for us to acknowledge these positive attributes, since those who opposed the project did not pay enough attention to its underlying aspects. Rather, they seem to have merely dismissed these, or worse, did not pursue them. Daya Krishna referred to two kinds of people who opposed to the project. Of them, he wrote, 'There are sceptics, as always, who doubt about the worth of the whole enterprise. There are others who believe that it is a movement positively in the wrong direction. For them, there is no need to resurrect the past or to make it alive. Let that which deserves to die, be allowed to die' (Ibid.: xv).

While Daya Krishna seems to have carefully classified the opponents of the project, there has been no scholarly response from the critics and sceptics he identified. This is disheartening. It is this tendency to leave philosophical positions at the level of opinions and private discussions, without carrying them forward into a scholarly discussion or debate that is a serious limitation, even a defect that undermines philosophy in contemporary India. Yet, while I acknowledge the positive facets of this project, what concerns me is the fact that the project did not learn certain important lessons from a similar project that had been launched previously. I have in mind the Jaipur experiment which I will describe below.

The Jaipur Experiment

The experiment aimed to establish an exchange of teachers between the Jaipur University philosophy department and the Sanskrit College in Jaipur city. However, says Daya Krishna, the philosophy teachers' proposal to teach courses in Western philosophy to their Sanskrit students has not been so successful as they do not seem to be interested in what we have to offer. However, he confirmed that their other experiment where they tried to establish a dialogue with some of the pandits in Varanasi, Calcutta, and Pune was successful, as the pandits there responded creatively. It is relevant to note here, however, that this enthusiasm seems to have been short-lived, as Daya Krishna subsequently referring to these attempts later reported that—'none of these had really clicked. They were good while they lasted. But they did not generate that feeling of discovery, enthusiasm and success [...] They were, so to say, abortive beginnings which did not lead to any successful fruition' (in his Introduction to Krishna et al. [1991: xii]). He repeats this in yet another place where specifying the time of the failure of Jaipur experiment he says, 'The Jaipur experiment lost its momentum sometime after 1985, and though occasional meetings of the group continued, we gradually began to realize that we could not proceed significantly beyond what had been achieved so far' (1996a: vii). Therefore, the Jaipur experiment did not bear long-term results, which was a serious problem. It was after this that the *Samvāda* project was initiated.

The Samvāda *Project*

Following this, an attempt by Rege resulted in the volume titled *Samvāda: A Dialogue between Two Philosophical Traditions* (Krishna et al. 1991).

This project, according to Daya Krishna, gave rise to some subsequent meetings such as on Nyāya (at Sarnath), on Mimāmsā (Tirupati), Saivism (Srinagar), and Islam (Aligarh). Apart from these, the project has not been pursued in a manner resulting in substantive philosophical debates rather than mere meetings. The reasons cited by Daya Krishna for the failure of the Jaipur experiment can be applied equally to the *Samvāda* project. Like the first, this too was not followed by serious and sustained efforts. The failure of these new and creative philosophical initiatives calls for serious introspection. As has already been pointed out, an important limitation underlying this project was that just as in the attempts of Matilal and others, here too the discussion was largely between classical Indian philosophy and contemporary Western philosophy. *Samvāda* largely focused on debating Russell's theory of the nature of propositions against Nyāya and Mimāmsā.

Let me now bring into our discussion some other limitations that constrain this project. In the context of making out a case for *Samvāda*, Rege identifies two parallel lines taken in Indian philosophical activity. The first one was concerned to 'participate in the on-going western philosophical debate and thus contribute to its progress'. This, Rege pointed out, is from the Western point of view, a 'contribution ... [that is] only ... marginal'. The other form of philosophical activity 'was addressed to the explication of the concepts and the exegesis of the theories of the Indian schools. These were exercises in the history of philosophy'. However, the problem with these two kinds of activities is that they 'remained apart'. Rege noted that '[t]here was never an interplay of western and Indian philosophical ideas' (Krishna et al. 1991: xx). In this context, he identified three interrelated issues, one of them being the reference to the term 'philosopher' in contemporary India. He wrote—

When one talks of Indian philosophers one has in mind western-trained Indian philosophers. But there has always been in India a countrywide community of philosophers, who worked within the Indian tradition and were engaged in formulating, criticising and reformulating philosophical theories through the medium of Sanskrit. This is the community of pandits or *Śāstris*. But they were never counted as philosophers ... they were regarded as scholars and not as philosophers. (Krishna et al. 1991: xx–xxi)

Thus, there is a problem with the term philosopher. It refers only to Western-trained Indian philosophers and does not include the pandits. The latter, says Daya Krishna, carry on their intellectual activity in Sanskrit which is 'still the *living lingua franca* of traditional scholarship in India, that the only language in which intellectual dialogue can be carried on between these persons from different parts of India ...' (Ibid.: xi). Thus, Sanskrit as the medium of philosophizing is the second issue.

The third issue brought into the discussion by Rege concerns various forms of Vedānta. While Western-trained Indian philosophers were hardly aware of the existence of various schools of Indian philosophy, however, says Rege, there 'was indeed one area of traditional Indian philosophy which was cultivated by many western-trained Indian philosophers as philosophy and not merely studied from a western historical perspective, that is various forms of *Vedānta*' (Ibid.: xxii).

So, pandits are not recognized as philosophers in India; second, they discuss philosophy in Sanskrit; and lastly, various forms of Vedānta are recognized as philosophy by Western-trained philosophers. Let me address these three issues, which, we recall, are mentioned by Rege in the context of the problem of the absence of interaction between the two types of philosophical activities. I agree with the criticism that the term 'philosopher' is used too narrowly in contemporary India, and, further, that pandits ought to be included within the term philosophers. However, another group of philosophers, who are our immediate predecessors, seems to have eluded the attention of Daya Krishna and Rege, namely, Swami Vivekananda, Sri Aurobindo, and Mahatma Gandhi. This group does not fall either into the category of academic, Western-trained philosophers or into the category of pandits. I will justify my decision to bring this third group of philosophers into the discussion. But before I do that, let me clarify that while there is perhaps a need to facilitate the use of Sanskrit as a medium of philosophizing, there is also a serious attempt being undertaken to practice Indian philosophy in English, without the use of Sanskrit, which involves complex layers of translation of ideas. (For more on this, see Mehta's interpretation of Krishna Chandra Bhattacharyya 1974). Also, while Rege is right in distinguishing schools of Vedānta from other philosophical schools, and establishing that it is considered legitimate philosophy by Western-trained philosophers, he fails to explain why this philosophical school, that is, Vedānta, acquired its singular status.

While accepting that modern Western philosophers have given no reason for rejecting classical Indian philosophy, as they have in the case of classical Western philosophy, an anomaly mentioned by Sudipto Kaviraj (2005: 133), what cannot be forgotten is the fact that there is an antagonistic relation between modern and classical philosophy. So, to make a plea, or propose, to modern Western philosophers, that they take into account classical Indian philosophy, would be too naïve an idea. Yet this is precisely what is proposed by the *Samvāda* project. What is, however, possible, is to contest the antagonistic relation that presently obtains between the classical and the modern. This is what is undertaken by philosophers such as Swami Vivekananda, Sri Aurobindo, and Krishna Chandra Bhattacharyya. Once this antagonism or disjunction between the classical and the contemporary is diminished, this can pave the way for a proposal to accept pandits as philosophers. Without preparing this ground it would be unrealistic to make such a proposition. Unlike modern Western philosophers like Descartes, who suggested that the entirety of the past ought to be rejected, contemporary Indian philosophers have come up with a new proposal wherein, in conjunction with the incorporation of many contemporary features, particularly those from modern science, several things from the past can also be recalled and retained in a positive manner. This is what underlies the proposition of a marriage between materialism (modern) and spiritualism (classical). In the context of propounding a synthesis between the West and the

East, Vivekananda claimed that Vedānta stood the present-day test of modern scientific reasoning. He said—'The Vedas teach us that creation is without beginning or end. Science is said to have proved that the sum total of cosmic energy is always the same' (Volume I, 1994: 7). According to him—'The religion of the Vedanta can satisfy the demands of the scientific world, by referring it to the highest generalisation and to the law of evolution. That the explanation of a thing comes from within itself is still more completely satisfied by Vedanta' (Volume I, 1994: 374).

He added further that '...the modern physical researches are tending more and more to demonstrate that what is real is but the finer; the gross is simply appearance... we have seen that if any theory of religion can stand the test of modern reasoning, it is the Advaita, because it fulfils its two requirements' (Volume I, 1994: 376).

This proposal of the modern contemporary Indian philosophers for a synthesis between classical Indian philosophy—in this case Vedānta—and modern science, rather than the rejection of the classical instituted by modern Western philosophers, provides a good foundation for facilitating the recognition of pandits as philosophers. However, the opportunity that these modern Indian philosophers, such as Vivekananda, provide, and their immense contribution have escaped the attention of the authors of the *Samvāda* project. There is no reference in the project to modern Indian philosophers. One might say that what pandits are to modern Western philosophers, contemporary Indian philosophers are to the philosophers of the *Samvāda* project. This project, in its enthusiasm for their ancestors, neglected their predecessors, an omission which costs them dearly. The neglect is particularly ironic, considering that the project is authored by those very philosophers who are making out a case for the victims of exclusion.

Aside from making out a case for modern Indian philosophers at the level of agency and their non-inclusion, they also, I maintain, are important for the following reasons—they initiated series of readjustments between the modern/colonial and the classical Indian; they also facilitated the change of deliberations from Sanskrit to English;

finally, they made a case for the urgent need to bring the 'masses' into the mainstream (for more on this, see Raghuramaraju 2011).

The recent attempts to revive Indian philosophy and helping it become equal to the weighty tasks assigned to it are marked by an unprecedented complexity, which involves making adjustments, changing the medium of expression, incorporating new interventions without at the same time surrendering entirely to them, admitting internal defects, suggesting mechanisms to overcome them, and making new proposals of synthesis between classical and modern, Eastern and Western. And it must be noted that though contemporary Indian philosophical thinking may not have succeeded in all these endeavours, they however did attempt to rise to the occasion. Thus, the remarkable feature of thinkers like Swami Vivekananda, Sri Aurobindo, and Krishna Chandra Bhattacharyya is that their efforts were informed by the contemporary political matrix dominated by colonialism and anti-colonial struggle, and they strove to connect the Indian and the Western, thereby avoiding the wholesale rejection of either. That is, while making out a case for Advaita, Swami Vivekananda did not repudiate modern Western materialism, nor did Sri Aurobindo deny Darwin's evolutionary theory completely. They only pointed out the limitations of Western thought. Their ingenuity lay in converting the Western binary opposition between religion and evolutionary theory into continuity. The form of Advaita that is presented by these thinkers is informed by contemporary developments which have saved it from becoming archaic.

Given the changing cultural and political scenario, these contemporary Indian philosophers have shown sensitivity in introducing a kind of philosophizing that attempted to negotiate developments in the West while making sense of the classical philosophy of India. I have pointed out how they shifted to the new language, namely, English, while managing not to remain insulated as did the academic philosophers whom Rege referred to. Taking note of the changes around them, those like Vivekananda did undertake the exercise of bringing the masses into the mainstream, an act that shows aspects of egalitarianism and a clear rejection of elitism in traditional

Indian philosophy. Unlike the insulation that Rege commented upon, the version of Advaita propounded by Vivekananda and others did not remain within the confined circles of the Sanskrit pandits. Rather, these philosophers made out a case for restating Advaita in the context of developments in modern science and philosophy. It is this that made Advaita respectable, in stark contrast to other schools of Indian philosophy. The problem with the *Samvāda* project is that, to begin with, it failed to take into consideration this group of philosophers and their specific contribution to relate the West, especially modern West with the classical Indian which included changing the medium of philosophizing, bringing the masses into the mainstream, and taking Advaita outside the confines of the pandits' circles. In other words, the criticism advocated by those from *Samvāda* project is not firmly grounded, and is not informed by already available discussions on the state of Indian philosophy. All these escaped the notice of the *Samvāda* project.

Instead, the project sought to revive the classical texts. That is, while the twentieth century is concerned with egalitarianism, the texts that the *Samvāda* project was recalling for discussion are elitist and exclusive. The time was ill suited to highlight their significance. While I do not think that classical texts ought to be rejected outright, I do think that they are on sabbatical. Here, I would like to clarify that being on sabbatical does not mean not doing philosophy. When one is on sabbatical, it means one does not or cannot teach in one's workplace, but continues philosophizing both outside and within the institution. Similarly, one can do Indian philosophy outside Sanskrit. To reiterate the limitation of the caution stated earlier, while classical texts can be used to elucidate concepts, categories, and modes of thought, it is necessary to remember that the time is not so propitious for these texts. Therefore, these classical texts need not be rejected, nor retired, nor exiled, but they can be sent on sabbatical. So there is a need to recognize the virtue of sleep, not merely see wakefulness on the one hand and death on the other. Sleep, which bridges wakefulness and death, has some useful figurative allusions that will be of immense help in formulating contemporary Indian philosophical concerns.

While the great contribution of Daya Krishna, Rege, and others lies in embarking on the philosophy of absence, namely, why there are no dialogues in Indian philosophy today when classical India is dialogical, the themes with which they sought to fill the absence had some serious limitations. The late nineteenth and twentieth centuries were very important for the practice of philosophy in India. Thinkers of this period actively and ingeniously negotiated with both classical Indian and modern Western thought in conjunction with colonialism and the struggle for Indian independence. Seeking to reach one's ancestors without recognizing one's predecessors is what costs the practice of philosophy in India dearly today. The next chapter elaborates further upon the degradations caused by this neglect through discussing yet another philosopher, K. Satchidananda Murty, who also neglects the contributions of these predecessors.

5

PHILOSOPHY IN INDIA

The relationship between philosophy and India in the contemporary period is complex. India is a cauldron of several interventions from the outside, in addition to an already existent plurality of classical philosophical systems. This complexity, however, has not translated into an advantage, and has so far remained disadvantageous. At the most it has become a de facto virtue of mere difference with regard to instances found in the West. One of the reasons for this is the lack of any relation between two or amongst more than two of its various parts. This superficial and continuous increase of volume, without simultaneously broadening the interactions, whether positive or negative, between or amongst systems, eventually became cumbersome.

In contrast to this contemporary situation, in the classical period, on the other hand, there existed in India a direct relation between or amongst different or various philosophical systems. For instance, the debate between Buddhism and Advaita, or between Buddhists and Nyāya. This has become a virtue, largely as a result of vital and up-to-date interactions between these systems. The peculiarity of the situation then was that the opponent of a system knew as much, if not more, about the system he was opposing as about his own. Thus, there were debates between two, or amongst more than two systems, and there was clarity about one's station and position in the debate. This allowed for clarity and vision amongst both followers and opposers of any system. Therefore, there was no difficulty in communicating matters related to one's system, and the primary preoccupation was with defending, critiquing, and evaluating one's own and others' systems. These actions are central to the quality of philosophical debate and require alertness and ingenuity rather than bearing the burden of one's own system.

A similar scene prevailed in the West with the advent of modernity. Modernity came with a clear critique of both Greek and Christian philosophies. With the formation of a clear methodology, it refuted, rejected, or even made out a case for disinheriting the past and pre-modern philosophies. As already discussed, this is clearly evident in Descartes, the father of modern Western philosophy. He used a unique logic of exclusion followed by inclusion, and embarked upon a massive project of excluding anything located in the pre-modern from the premises of the modern. Subsequently, Western philosophers attempted to bring some of those excluded by Descartes through the thematic of the modern, back into the modern. This task preoccupied Social Contract philosophers who parked the Cartesian cognitive nude in the imaginary state-of-nature. Hegel resurrected history, Darwin evolution, Marx social reality, and Freud unconsciousness, and the ordinary language philosophers resuscitated ordinary language. This was the fundamental and consistent project undertaken by the Western philosophers. There is an underlying chain of ideas that sustained philosophy in the West. The respect that the subject of philosophy received in the West, and its progress there, is not merely a result of the part of it concerned with application, or the speculative part, but because it judiciously and meticulously discharged this job of responding to the larger issues that are indispensable and irreplaceable.

In addition to this underlying chain of thought the other important feature of philosophy in the West is that whenever things were going out of control immediate measures were taken to correct them. Take for instance Husserl, who in his *Crisis of European Sciences and Transcendental Phenomenology* (1970) warns of the implications of excessive objectivism which may result in the virtual elimination of the subject or the self. In my view, he has reminded the project of modernity of how it instituted as its primary task the autonomy of the subject. It is the importance of this self that is becoming eroded with the advance of science. Using the philosophical gaze Husserl warns that modernity, which is given to excessive objectivism and faith in science, is unable to see, because of its micro-level involvement, the erosion of the self and subjectivity, and thereby of the human being that is its primary concern. Similarly, you have the democratic argument that underlies ordinary language philosophy. Logical positivism's scientifically oriented attempt to eliminate metaphysics and religion caused, as side effects, the rejection of ordinary language and replacement by artificial language. By implication, the ordinary which constitutes the core of democracy gets excluded or eliminated. The excess in this objectivism of logical positivism, and its implications to the 'ordinary' is pointed out later by Wittgenstein. It is this onerous task that made this brand of philosophy, that is, ordinary language philosophy, a respectable branch of philosophical activity. Consider also Alasdair MacIntyre's work, *After Virtue* (1985), in which he points out that excess of modern individualism leads to the unviability of consensus. I have taken those seemingly not so politically visible texts to show the kind of role philosophy has played in the West. As major figures in the field are performing this task of attending to larger issues, university departments, their research projects and publications, are continuously sharpening their tools by placing all their concepts, arguments, and systems under ever closer critical scrutiny. Philosophies in India, before the arrival of modernity, were also active and their positions were as clear as their interactions were regular. To quote Kalidas Bhattacharyya—

'[T]raditional Indian philosophy' is the corpus of philosophical doctrines and dissertations that have been current in India for at least two millenniums and communicated from generation to generation mainly through Sanskrit language and largely also through Pali ... and Prakrit.... The beauty of the whole tradition is that it was a perfectly living widespread study among Indian philosophers till only the other day—till, one may say, a hundred and twenty-five years back.... This was the case even during the whole period of Muslim rule in India. (1982: 171–2)

The current scene in India is different. In the context of elucidating this difference let me note two features about philosophy in the West. One, Western philosophy is truly substantial, and there is no doubt about its quality and extent. Yet, it is necessary to acknowledge at the same time, that there exists in the West a discontinuous relationship between the pre-modern and the modern. It may be noted, in fact, as I have argued elsewhere, that the term West was first used in the early nineteenth century (Raghuramaraju 2005). Thus, classifying Plato as a Western philosopher is anachronistic. Unlike the West, modern India does not have a discontinuous relationship with its past; on the contrary, modern Indian philosophers, while responding to modernity, simultaneously rewrote their traditional philosophy. This provides us with a different combination of modern and pre-modern to that in the West, what I am describing is a *sandhi* period. It is against this backdrop that I embark on a close reading of K. Satchidananda Murty's important work *Philosophy in India: Traditions, Teaching and Research.*

The work is a monumental report on the practice of philosophy in India. It gives the reader a broad spectrum view of philosophical practices in India. The first chapter presents a comprehensive idea of the different uses of philosophy in India, which include—*Brahmodaya, atmavidya, paravidya, Brahmavidya, mimāmsā, ditthi (dristi)*, and the destruction of ditthi leading to the birth of *prajña*. In this context, Murty points out how Nyāya, by bringing in critical scrutiny and a logical dimension, tried to save those systems that relied on scriptures. While discussing the various uses of philosophy, Murty writes—

From very ancient times dristi meant philosophic view, theory or opinion. The Jainas too adapted this word. For example, Siddhasena Divākara of the fifth century A.D. said: In Jina coalesce all dristis as all rivers in the ocean. Haribhadra (eighth century A.D.), author of the earliest available compendium on different philosophical systems,

used darsana to mean a philosophic system and titled his book 'A
Compendium of Six Philosophies' (*Sad-darśana-samuccaya*). Since
then this word gained vogue with this meaning, and when Mādhava,
a famous Vedāntic thinker of the fourteenth century A.D., titled his
work giving summaries of fifteen philosophic systems *Sarvadarśana
Sangraha* ('A Summary of all Philosophic Systems'), darśana there-
after became the most popular word to denote a philosophic system,
though other words like *prasthāna*, *tarka* and *tantra* too were used to
denote philosophical systems. (1985: 6–7)

A notable feature of Murty's conclusion is its comprehensiveness.
He highlights clearly, and strikingly, Jainism's contribution to the
consolidation of the various systems of Indian philosophy under a
single umbrella of *syadvada* doctrine. Mallavadi of the fifth century,
writes Murty, 'conceived all standpoints (nayas) as converging in the
theory of relativity (syādvāda), because Truth is many-sided, comparing them to the spoke of a wheel coming from the felly (sic) converging
in the naval' (1985: 7). The point skillfully blends relativism with pluralism. Here, Murty brings into the discussion an observation made
by Manibhadra, the commentator of *Haribhadra*, that—'Buddhism
can be heard, Jaina dharma performed, Vaidika dharma adhered to,
and the supreme Śiva meditated upon' (1985: 7–8). Murty adds that
the Nyaya thinker Udayana had tried to show the non-opposition of
different philosophical systems to each other. This was also endorsed
by Abhinavagupta, leader of the Kashmir Saiva School.

There are two other important points that Murty makes in this
context. He writes that mutually contradictory philosophical positions cannot be resolved; therefore, the right path, according to the
Mahabharata, is the one that is followed by *mahajana*, which can
mean both the 'great or distinguished men', and also 'many people,
multitude of men' (1985: 7). The second point Murty makes about
the various philosophical *darsana*s, or systems, invoked the sixteenth
century Advaitin thinker Madhusudhana Saraswati who explained that
different systems of philosophy were offered so as 'to appeal to all kinds
of men' (1985: 8). The important aspect of Murty's first chapter is its
foregrounding of the entire subsequent debate over philosophy in India.

Murty's next chapter discusses the history of philosophical thinking in India, including the Vedas, Upanishads, Jainism, Lokayata, Buddhism including Sthaviravada, Sarvastivada, Sautrantika, Mahasanghika, and Vignanavada, the epic Mahabharata, the Gita, the Hindu darsanas comprising Sankhya-Yoga, Nyāya-Vaiseshika, Purva, and Uttara Mimāmsā, the latter incorporating within it post-Sankara Vedānta. The appendix to the chapter describes the vital relationship between classical practices, as presented in *Haribhadra* and *Machala*, which, Murty writes, was 'established with the publication of the first volume of Dasgupta's *History* and Radhakrishnan's two volumes' (1986: 45). Murty explains that in these two books, each system

> ... is treated as finished organic whole from the beginning with an epistemology, metaphysics and ethics.... The genesis and the growth of ideas in each, their correlation with intellectual and material conditions around, the contributions of individual thinkers, and the factors that influenced them, their mutual interaction, etc. do not find a place either in teaching or in text-books used. (1985: 45)

I will closely analyse this passage as it forms the basis for Murty's subsequent discussion. The problems with these seminal books by Radhakrishnan and Dasgupta are as follows—first, they treat each system as a finished organic whole. Second, they do not identify the genesis of each system, trace the growth of ideas within it, or point out how the systems were correlated with the intellectual and material conditions that surrounded them. More importantly, in Murty's reckoning, these books did not clarify the contributions of individual thinkers, the factors that influenced them, and their mutual interactions. These shortcomings are the major problems surrounding both the method of instruction and the textbooks used in the teaching of the history of Indian philosophy in Indian universities. The overall scenario described, in terms of textbooks and teaching, has largely prevailed in India, despite a few exceptions. These include, for example, Dasgupta's account of individual thinkers' contributions in some systems, particularly the three Vedantic systems, and of the controversies that arose amongst thinkers of different schools.

There is also D. D. Kosambi's work tracing the rise and development of Buddhism, G. C. Pande's analysis of the social and ideational foundations of Indian culture, and the scholarly work of the Marxist philosopher D. P. Chattopadhyaya. Even so, as Murty writes, these 'do not trace the logical development of ideas within each school, stage by stage' (1985: 46). Also, notwithstanding these, Murty reminds us, in Indian universities—'... due to the prestige of Radhakrishnan and Dasgupta, [theirs] became the accepted approach to the history of Indian philosophy, and consequently no attempt to write a real history of Indian philosophy as a whole has been made in India since their time' (1985: 47).

In this context, Murty does acknowledge some exceptions to this mainstream as available in the works of M. N. Roy, Rahul Sankrityayana, D. P. Chattopadhyaya, K. Damodaran, Pandit Sukhlal*ji*, and his own work which trace the development of ideas within systems logically and stage by stage.

The next chapter titled 'History of Philosophical Thinking in India II', brings into discussion contributions outside of formal and disciplinary domains, especially those drawn from the religio-philosophical literatures of the Dravidian, Apabhramsa, and modern Indo-Aryan languages, from the sixth century AD. Murty discusses Tamil mysticism, Saiva Siddhanta, *Kural* ethics, the Sahajiya and Siddhas, the Nayathas, Vira Saiva, Sarvajna, the Bhakti movement from Maharashtra, mysticism and egalitarianism from Andhra, popular Kashmiri syntheses, north Indian *sant*s and *bhakta*s, Sikhism, late medieval Vaishnava movement, the Bauls, and Indo-Muslim philosophy. The fourth chapter discusses philosophy in modern India. Murty writes that the author of *Mahanirvana Tantra*, written between 1775 and 1785, may be regarded as the father of modern Indian philosophy. According to him, this text

... is the greatest religio-philosophical work of the eighteenth century. It attempted to expound a monotheistic reformed religion and was also intended to be used as a law book. It permitted widow remarriage, and interdining and intermarriage amongst all who accepted its doctrines and joined its brotherhood founded on the spiritual practice it prescribed. It advocated the abolition of food taboos, *sati* ... and slavery. Hariharānanda, the guru of Rammohun Roy, wrote a commentary on it, and the latter's reform movement derived inspiration from it. (1985: 97–98)

In chapter 4 of his book, Murty merely mentions the names of philosophers from outside the domain of the university, such as Ram Mohan Roy, Swami Dayananda, Narayana Guru, Swami Rama Tirtha, Bal Gangadhar Tilak, and Mohammad Iqbal. However, he fails to capture the essential contributions of these modern Indian thinkers. From within the university, the names mentioned are Brajendranath Seal, S. N. Dasgupta, S. Radhakrishnan, R. D. Ranade, and Hiralal Haldar. Subsequent parts of the chapter briefly discuss the works of Indian philosophers of the nineteenth and early twentieth centuries. Murty discusses Vivekananda, Tagore, Gandhi, Sri Aurobindo, Radhakrishnan, Krishna Chandra Bhattacharyya, Iqbal, and Indian Christian and Parsi philosophers. In the appendix to this chapter, he analyses the contribution of modern writing in Indian languages, and concludes that 'the quality and quantity of the work done in Indian languages is not in any way inferior to that done by Indians in English, and in some cases distinctly superior to the latter' (1985: 120).

The fifth chapter elucidates the present philosophical situation in the country. It contains reports on teaching and research in philosophy in different regions of the country, written by G. C. Nayak, E. I. Warrier, S. S. Barlingay, Arjun Misra, Ashok Vohra, Sibajiban Bhattacharyya, R. Balasubramanian, Sangam Lal Pandeya, and Kireet Joshi. In addition to this, Murty mentions the *Poona Report* prepared by Bokil and Barlingay which is extremely critical of the teaching and research being done in India. The report, says Murty,

... comments that as in certain universities there is a total absence of researches in logic, their researches in other areas (e.g. metaphysics and moral philosophy) have no strong logical base; and that as in most departments there is a total absence of research in philosophy of science, especially of social sciences, they may not be able to make any creative advance in their researches in areas like philosophy of religion. The report also observes that contemporary Indian philosophy is being mostly studied in 'a disjointed and sporadic manner', most theses in this area being only 'descriptive-historical.' It concludes that in India there 'does not seem to be any meaningful and significant pattern of research ', that much of the work in moral and social philosophy is 'likely to be imprecise and loose' because of lack of contact with logic and theory of knowledge, and that most of the work in all areas has only a descriptive orientation. (1985: 132 and 134)

In commenting on the *Poona Report*, Murty leaves coming to any conclusions vis-à-vis the report, to the reader. He writes—

While the value of the *Poona Report* is undeniable, its presuppositions and conclusions may not be acceptable to all. The readers may also decide for themselves what are the important new facts, if any, brought to light by this report, and whether its analysis and conclusions differ significantly from those contained in the introductions to the collected volumes mentioned earlier. (1985: 134)

While the fifth chapter dealt with the state of philosophy in the different regions of the country, the next, and sixth, chapter explores notes prepared at the request of the author by five philosophers about the 'general philosophical situation at present, the problems of the profession and future prospects for philosophy in India' (1985: 137). The five philosophers in question are Kalidas Bhattacharyya, Syed Vahiduddin, Santosh Sengupta, Waheed Akhtar, and Suresh Chandra. The central 'problems of the profession', as reported, could be summed up under the following heads—that the number of students seeking admission in philosophy was 'small', the quality of students 'relatively inferior', departments were closed down and teachers' contracts terminated [without] appropriate legal notice, employment opportunities were limited, there was little scope for expansion and growth, and the number of scholarly journals was negligible. Murty reports what appeared to be almost a consensus in the profession that these core problems could be solved by 'increased financial assistance and expansion of employment opportunities'. Thus, Murty concluded—'To sum up, it seems to be the general impression that in contemporary India philosophy as it is pursued in universities and colleges ... is not considered important and is not encouraged' (1985: 144).

He also notes the criticism that 'University philosophy' did not cater to the needs of the people; unlike the philosophy of holy men or sages, academic philosophy is removed from reality. Yet, while acknowledging the truth of the criticisms that were made, Murty also recognizes the great and intrinsic value of 'university philosophy' (1985: 148). He thus concludes the chapter by declaring that the lack of 'courage of conviction and lethargy among professional philosophers are the only obstacle to the rectification of philosophy in India' (1985: 156).

It is evident from the discussion of K. Satchidananda Murty's seminal work that his was a colossal task, undertaken by one of the leading philosophers of India. The scope of the book is broad, and the different parts are comprehensively covered. The work testifies to the author's ingenuity and range of scholarship. A well-known scholar of classical Indian and Western philosophy, with a deep knowledge of Sanskrit, Murty was nonetheless never lost in the supposed otherworldliness of the subject nor did he allow technical details to blur his vision. Murty was perhaps one of the few philosophers who had from the very beginning an inclination towards classical Indian philosophy, and yet he could both understand and appreciate the materialist schools of philosophy, and particularly recent works from these schools. This is evident in his valuation of the scholarship of Rahul Sankrityayana, D. D. Kosambi, and D. P. Chattopadhyaya.

Murty regarded with equal admiration the work of Sikh, Muslim, Christian, and Parsi philosophers in India. Chapter 3 of his book is a testimony to his work towards broadening the contours of philosophy so that they might include contributions from more marginal areas such as mysticism, and the bhakti movement. His attitude is at once challenging and liberating for some of us who have faced academic fundamentalists in philosophy, who ordained, for example, that political philosophy cannot count as philosophy. A fundamentalist is one who understands little of the doctrine yet seriously seeks to enforce it. Murty has become a source of comfort to academic refugees who have been displaced by the fundamentalists.

Murty is perhaps the only philosopher who is interested in Advaita philosophy, yet remains aware of the cultural, materialist basis of this idealist school of thought. This is one of the reasons why he is critical of S. Radhakrishnan's and S. N. Dasgupta's works on Indian philosophy, but finds the work of G. C. Pande on Buddhism, and that of Jainism expert Pandit Sukhla*ji* in his work *Indian Philosophy*, both remarkable and important. In Murty, we find an idealist philosopher who knows the importance of materialism; he is also the one thinker who represents many different aspects of secular India. Finally, the scholarship presented in the book provides students of philosophy with an impressive and comprehensive reading list which can remove any doubts about the richness and depth of Indian philosophy.

Having said all this let me now delineate the limitations of this work. A major weakness of the work is its inability to adjudicate between admitting the pitiable condition of what he calls 'university philosophy' while still recognizing the rich resources that are available. Two reasons identified by Murty for the generally poor quality of 'university philosophy' are lack of funding and few employment opportunities. But these are less the causes of the problem than the effects of the situation. Moreover, it may be seen that the high levels of funding available for philosophy in IITs and Central universities have not improved the situation of philosophy in these institutions. In this context, we may discuss an interesting passage in Murty's book. While discussing the nature and extent of philosophy as praxis, he writes in relation to an important characteristic of philosophical practice in the West—

Dante and Holderlin were not philosophers, but what Santayana and Heidegger did on them is philosophy; the outpourings of the mystics,

whether of the East or the West, may not be philosophy, but what
Bergson, Royce, Hocking and Stace wrote on them is philosophy;
and while history and historiography are not philosophy, the thinking
of Dilthey and Croce on them is philosophy. (1985: 178–9)

The importance of this passage lies in the recognition of a task of
philosophy which is different than its usual tasks. While philosophy
proposes a system, and rigorously analyses it, it is an entirely different
matter to make philosophy out of non-philosophical material. Yet this
is what was undertaken by Sankara, Plato, Nagarjuna, St. Thomas
Aquinas, St. Augustine, and many others. What is important now in
India is to use resources available not only within philosophy, but
also outside it, and to make a philosophical system, or systems, anew.
There is an immediate need to seriously reassess modern Indian
philosophers such as Vivekananda, Aurobindo, Gandhi, and Krishna
Chandra Bhattacharyya, and to construct philosophical systems from
their ideas, kindling fresh interest in these thinkers by generating new
debates around their philosophical oeuvres. This is a rare opportunity that is given to philosophers in India, since contemporary India
is a confluence of classical Indian and modern Western—a unique
conjunction that the West cannot occupy or access. Yet it is, without
doubt, an enormous task.

The justification for making the claim that these predecessors
ought to be reincorporated into our current philosophical thinking
is not merely notional but substantial. I make two points in relation to this—First, identify the rich resources that are available in
these thinkers. And, next, find ways of making the best use of these
resources. For instance, let us address Sri Aurobindo. In the following
passage he shows sensitivity to both classical Indian philosophy and
the new thinking brought by modernity, and attempts to negotiate
both trajectories of thought. He writes—

We have practically to take three facts into consideration, the great
past of Indian culture and life with the moment of inadaptive torpor
into which it has lapsed, the first period of the Western contact in
which it seemed for a moment likely to perish by slow decomposition,

and the ascending movement which first broke into some clarity of
expression only a decade or two ago... Indian spirituality ... has
always maintained itself even in the decline of the national vitality; it
was certainly that which saved India always at every critical moment
of her destiny, and it has been the starting-point too of her renascence.
Any other nation under the same pressure would have long ago per-
ished soul and body. But certainly the outward members were becoming gangrened; the powers of renovation seemed for a moment to be
beaten by the powers of stagnation, and stagnation is death. Now that
the salvation, the reawakening has come, India will certainly keep her
essential spirit, will keep her characteristic soul, but there is likely to
be a great change of the body. The shaping for itself of a new body,
of new philosophical, artistic, literary, cultural, political, social forms
by the same soul rejuvenescent will, I should think, be the type of
the Indian renascence,—forms not contradictory of the truths of life
which the old expressed, but rather expressive of those truths restated,
cured of defect, completed. (In Bhushan and Garfied 2011: 40–1)

Aurobindo in this passage clearly captures various aspects associated with the modern Indian situation, particularly, the diagnosis of
the problems, limitations within Indian thought, and the scope for
improvement.

The central issue with Murty's work is that, being primarily preoccupied with university philosophy, it makes an index of contributions
that lie outside the subject but fails to analyse them. It was perhaps
not possible for him to have undertaken such an analysis given the
nature of his work, however, we may yet use his discussion as a
stepping place to extend its scope further. There is a need to scru-
tinize the success and failure of the various attempts to reinvigorate
philosophical activity in India. How, for instance, did the works of
Swami Vivekananda, Sri Aurobindo, Mahatma Gandhi, and even
Krishna Chandra Bhattacharyya receive positive attention, or critical
scrutiny? And what are the limitations of the attempts of others, such
as B. K. Matilal, J. N. Mohanty, Daya Krishna? (Incidentally, Murty
does not mention the work of an important contemporary philosopher, J. L. Mehta. This is surprising as he too was interested in the

Vedas and Hermeneutics). Therefore, we have an opportunity to do what Santayana, Heidegger, Bergson, Royce, Hocking, and Stace did in the West, and in so doing, revivify philosophy in India.

Another important limitation of Murty's work is that while elucidating the state of philosophy in India, he does not give careful consideration to the actual state of philosophy in the West as compared to their other disciplines. The situation of philosophy in the West is less good than might be expected, since several branches have been declared dead, including ethics, metaphysics, and even political philosophy in some places. Recognizing this flaw might have given us some relief, if only through a vicarious awareness of their gloomy situation. Let me also add that there are many philosophers in the West who have regarded Indian philosophy in a positive light, including modern Indian philosophers such as S. Radhakrishnan. Alasdair MacIntyre in his *Short History of Ethics* (2002) laments how much the West has missed or lost by not seriously engaging with Eastern philosophies. Taking into account their ordeals and their recognition of our virtues would have given us more courage to march ahead.

I will extend this discussion by bringing into it two further related points. First, I think that one of the chief obstacles that loom before philosophers in India is not their understanding of Indian philosophy, or lack thereof, but their misunderstanding of Western philosophy, or the West. The West is not a monolith with which we can compare Indian philosophy as a whole. In actual fact, there is a deep discontinuity between the classical and the modern in the West. The West, as a cultural term, was of a recent origin and was used notably in Spengler's *The Decline of the West* (1991). As previously mentioned, placing Plato in the *History of Western Philosophy* is akin to claiming that one was present at one's mother's marriage. The notion of a heterogeneous West also provides us with further emotional and intellectual incentives to improve the condition of philosophy in India. Despite the existence of so much learning, teaching, and research by philosophers in India, their understanding has to a great extent become trapped in the mastering of fragments of a technique, while failing to grasp the greater philosophical and civilizational nuances and complexities of Western culture and philosophy/philosophies. This is very disappointing.

Let me take this opportunity to make another point. One can sense in Murty's work that he holds S. Radhakrishnan responsible for presenting an ahistorial view of the different philosophical systems. While agreeing with Murty on this issue in Radhakrishnan's work, where I diverge from him is on the question of why this should stop the reader from reading the many other books available on Indian philosophy? My perspective on the matter is that I do not think we have read Radhakrishnan seriously. Had we read his works seriously, their limitations would have driven us to read other books. Therefore, my hunch is that we might have bought Radhakrishnan's books but I am not sure if we have read them; that is, read them with due care and seriousness. On the contrary, the elevated value that the subject of philosophy received as a result of Radhakrishnan's work and his career is enormous, and we have not kept pace with it. If our inability to keep pace with it is due to the extended elevation set by Radhakrishnan then that is another matter. India chose a philosopher as its president. I think there are several sub-texts behind this choice which need to be decoded. Moreover, the recognition given to him was not sudden. He was consistently promoted as if he had been continuously evaluated. Thus, India did not fail in recognizing the value of philosophy. If there is a problem with the subject, then it must lie somewhere other than in the worth given to it by the nation.

To continue this discussion, let us recall the pitiable situation of Indian philosophy in Radhakrishnan. He writes, as early as in the Preface to the First Edition of his *Indian Philosophy*—

Ignorance of the subject of Indian thought is profound. To the modern mind Indian philosophy means two or three 'silly' notions about *māyā*, or the delusiveness of the world, *karma*, or belief in fate, and *tyāga*, or the ascetic desire to be rid of the flesh. Even these simple notions, it is said, are wrapped up in barbarious nomenclature and chaotic clouds of vapour and verbiage, looked upon by the 'natives' as wonders of intellect. After a six-months' tour from Calcutta to Cape Comorin, our modern aesthete dismisses the whole of Indian culture and philosophy as 'pantheism,' 'worthless scholasticism,' 'a mere play upon words,' 'at all events nothing similar to Plato or Aristotle, or even Plotinus or Bacon.' (2008: xi)

Against this unpromising backdrop, Radhakrishnan goes on to claim the importance of Indian philosophy, thereby rejecting the existing state of things, and states—

The intelligent student interested in philosophy will, however, find in Indian thought an extraordinary mass of material which for detail and variety has hardly any equal in any other part of the world. There is hardly any height of spiritual insight or rational philosophy attained in the world that has not its parallel in the vast stretch that lies between the early Vedic seers and the modern Naiyāyikas.... The naïve utterances of the Vedic poets, the wondrous suggestiveness of the Upaniṣads, the marvellous psychological analyses of the Buddhists, and the stupendous system of Śaṃkara, are quite as interesting and instructive from the cultural point of view as the systems of Plato and Aristotle, or Kant and Hegel, if only we study them in a true scientific frame of mind, without disrespect for the past or contempt for the alien. (2008: xi–xii)

While making out a case for placing Indian philosophy at par with Western philosophy, I think that Radhakrishnan recommended a healthy attitude of neither disrespecting the past nor showing contempt for the alien, in pursuing the proper path. Conceding a contingent relationship between Indian thought and culture, Radhakrishnan claims that—'Even if Indian thought be not valuable from the cultural point of view, it is yet entitled to consideration, if on no other ground, at least by reason of its contrast to other thought systems and its great influence over the mental life of Asia' (2008: xii).

Having made this systematic and cumulative case for Indian philosophy, Radhakrishnan goes on to identify the aim of his book as being not merely to 'narrate' Indian views, but to 'explain them within the focus of Western traditions of thought' (2008: xiii). Murty's criticism of Radhakrishnan has to be evaluated against the stated aim of Radhakrishnan's book which is not to narrate the details of Indian philosophy to Indians. Rather his purpose is to make out a case for the very existence of Indian philosophy against those who claimed that there is no philosophy in India.

Thus, understanding the nature of philosophy in India is a complex task. This complexity can become a rich resource, and, as in the present situation, it can also lead to confusion. Ours is what I call a *sandhi* period, and an important characteristic of this period is the opportunity offered to negotiate between or amongst different, even incompatible, discourses; and the capability it bestows, of displaying dexterity in translating conflicting ideas, ideals, or proposals, to arrive at transformed, or better understanding. Through it we gain the ability to offer different settlements and make a variety of adjustments to respond to the local and communicate to the global. I suggest that we be at once logically rigorous and strong in our arguments, and yet sustain a larger perspective.

Here, we may draw out further Murty's contribution to our investigation of Indian philosophy, through his work, and, by way of thickening the plot as it were, avoid the ambivalence that is there in his book *Philosophy in India*. There is also a need to fill a gap, in addition to taking into account the contribution of the modern Indian thinkers mentioned earlier, that is to also consider the work done in institutions like the Centre for Philosophy in Amalner, where some of the stalwarts of Indian philosophy worked, including Krishna Chandra Bhattacharyya who wrote his famous *The Subject as Freedom* there, G. R. Malkani, and Ras Bihari Das. The present *Indian Philosophical Quarterly* that is now published from the University of Pune was started in Amalner. Murty's work does not adequately recognize the significant contributions of these kinds of centres.

Murty's work provides a vast, wonderful canvas. However, the internal dynamics between or amongst the various streams, and many contributions that remain unconnected to the mainstream, are largely left unremarked upon, or merely reported, by the author. In this, Murty's approach is similar to Radhakrishnan's, which Murty nonetheless criticizes. Given the existence of isolated, fragmentary, and seemingly unrelated works in the field, we find that there is an imperative need to connect them. The contributions of modern Indian thinkers from the nineteenth and twentieth centuries, which are already accessible to us, must be reclaimed by current academic discourse. The plea to bring these back in to the present philosophical mainstream is not made in order to accommodate the work of these thinkers because of their identity, and their importance in the freedom struggle, as may appear to be the case in books on contemporary Indian philosophy or courses offered in Indian universities. They must be brought back in because they have genuinely engaged in a sensitive, unrepetitive, if not creative way, with classical Indian philosophy. In other words, we need to recognize our predecessors before we approach our ancestors, and this is precisely because the former have already engaged with the latter.

In the last two chapters, I have examined two important philosophers who neglected their immediate predecessors and consequently achieved not very fruitful results. The next part consists of two chapters. They examine Coomaraswamy and Radhakrishnan's respective denials of the differences between Hinduism and Buddhism. The second chapter of this part also brings into the discussion B. R. Ambedkar and T. R. V. Murti, to reinvigorate the debate within both philosophical and political realms.

III

Denying the Difference

6

BUDDHISM IN HINDUISM

One way of reading Ananda Kenneth Coomaraswamy is to locate him within contemporary Indian philosophy. Although, like many others, he has written extensively on art and aesthetics, Coomaraswamy is also responding, albeit often indirectly, and I venture to say, imaginatively, to various views present all around him. And the views which surround him are corpus of complex and unclassified material, comprising classical Indian philosophy, Greek philosophy and art, colonialism, and modernity. Coomaraswamy's own ideas and observations, which are in part substantive responses to these views, reveal interesting relationships that are novel in nature. In this chapter, I will confine myself to Coomaraswamy's *Essays in National Idealism*, in which he proposes a unique version of nationalism. To lay bare the content of this uniqueness let me begin by asking, what is a nation?

One answer to this question is an essentialist one. We have a definition of a nation, and then there are different kinds of nations, say, a Western nation, the Indian nation, and so on. However, interestingly, this trajectory is not followed in the broader discussions on nationalism. On the other hand, Partha Chatterjee has asserted that the idea of the nation is taken from the Western idea of the nation, and therefore Indian nationalism is derivative. Chatterjee explains how Bankim, Gandhi, and Nehru laid the path to the making of the Indian nation.

Modern Indian philosophers, while making out a case for the nation, have invoked the past, and this has escaped the notice of

Partha Chatterjee.[1] Let me begin with the long quotation from Coomaraswamy where, in defiance of the basic tenets of Western nationalism, he clearly calls upon the past and claims it to be the constitutive factor in Indian nationalism. In the chapter titled 'Music and Education in India', he says—

> The essential error in modern Indian education, as understood by Government, missionaries, and Anglicised Indians, is a refusal or inability to recognize any responsibility to the past. The consequent break in the continuity of the historical tradition is fatal to Indian culture. It is much as if the caretakers of some ancient building, of complex origin, and various ages, hitherto accustomed to make additions and enlargements where and when required, had suddenly abandoned this process of development, in order to pull down the whole building, with the intention of rebuilding it upon a new plan, with the result that most of their energies became occupied with the provision of temporary huts for the inhabitants of the old house thus turned out into the cold. While scarcely any time was thus left for the serious work of reconstruction, and the needs of the day continued to grow faster than ever before, it would not have been surprising if some of the builders and their critics had regretted their haste in abandoning the old building, and reflected that their labours would have been better directed in building a new wing worthy of the old, than in pulling down what already existed. This is in fact just what is happening in India to-day; the destructive rather than constructive character of much of the education given in Indian schools and colleges is being recognized, but so slowly, that it is an open question whether any part of the old structure can be saved, to witness that the ancient builders builded well.
>
> Take music as a single case. (1981: 186–7)

Specifying the contents of his version of nationalism, at the very outset, Coomaraswamy clarifies that the essays in his book actually represent an endeavour towards an explanation of the true significance of the national movement in India. The significance of this movement for him can only be rightly understood, and ultimately has importance, 'only, as an idealistic movement'. He makes a distinction between the 'outward manifestations' of this movement and the 'deeper meaning of the struggle'. He alleges that the former had attracted 'abundant notice' whereas the latter is 'sometimes forgotten' both in 'England and in India' (1981: i). Coomaraswamy claims that if the deeper meaning of struggle is understood, not only by the world in general, but even by a large portion of the English, then 'people would extend to India a true sympathy in her life and death struggle with an alien bureaucracy' (1981: i). This 'struggle is much more than a political conflict. It is a struggle for spiritual and mental freedom from the domination of an alien ideal'. Thus, 'political and economic victory are but half the battle', and is only freedom in 'name'. The inner and deeper struggle is against the 'moral and spiritual subjection of Indian civilisation ...'. This spiritual subjection of Indian civilization, Coomaraswamy claims, 'in the end impoverishes humanity' (1981: i). Warning against those who get carried away by externalities and are unable to see the deeper meaning of the national struggle he writes—'So long as Indians are prepared to accept an education the aim of which is to make them English in all but colour—and at present they do in the main accept such education—they cannot achieve a national unity' (1981: iv).

Making a slight detour from his emphasis on the spiritual and religious, Coomaraswamy later declared that the material and the spiritual were inseparable. He wrote—

> The vital forces associated with the national movement in India are not merely political, but moral, literary, and artistic; and their significance lies in the fact that India henceforth will, in the main, judge all things by her own standards and from her own point of view. But the two sides of the national movement, the material and the spiritual, are inseparable, and must attain success or fail together. (1981: iv)

In addition to highlighting the need to understand the deeper struggle underneath rather than participating in a movement that would result in the victor voluntarily offering freedom, Coomaraswamy brings into the discussion the point of view that the Indian freedom struggle is not for the sake of a partisan interest confined to India, since, as he says, it 'is not out of hatred for England that India demands her freedom'. To the contrary, he declares that 'it is partly for England's sake', since the 'ownership of India is a chain about England's neck,—a weight not less hurtful because scarcely felt as such' (1981: vi). Thus, a deeper understanding of the struggle and the self-interest of the master were the two important aspects, according to Coomaraswamy, that would get India its independence.

Besides India and England, the victim and the victor, Coomaraswamy brought yet another variable into the discussion. I will quote him to show how he does this. Coomaraswamy writes that the 'inspiration of our Nationalism must be not hatred or self-seeking' but one must be based on 'Love, first of India, and secondly of England and of the World' (1981: viii). Then, if India did not win freedom then it would be bad for England and indeed the world, thereby greatly increasing the potential beneficiaries of the Indian freedom struggle. Why is Coomaraswamy justified in bringing the world into the picture? Because, for him, the

> ... highest ideal of nationality is service; and it is because this service is impossible for us so long as we are politically and spiritually dominated by any Western civilisation, that we are bound to achieve our freedom. It is in this spirit that we must say to Englishmen, that we will achieve this freedom, if they will, with their consent and with their help; but if they will not, then without their consent and in spite of their resistance. (1981: viii–ix)

Explaining the difference between imperialism and nationalism, Coomaraswamy writes that '... imperialism involves the subordination of many nationalities to one; a subordination not merely political and economic, but also moral and intellectual'.

Nationalism, on the other hand, he explains,

> is inseparable from the idea of Internationalism, recognising the rights and worth of other nations to be even as one's own. For Britain

we cannot speak; but for ourselves, the ideal is that of Nationalism and Internationalism. We feel that loyalty for us consists in loyalty to the idea of an Indian nation, politically, economically and intellectually free; that is, we believe in India for the Indians; but if we do so, it is not merely because we want our own India for ourselves, but because we believe that every nation has its own part to play in the long tale of human progress, and that nations, which are not free to develop their own individuality and own character, are also unable to make the contribution to the sum of human culture which the world has a right to expect of them. (1981: 2)

Bringing in a beautiful analogy to highlight the variability amongst cultures, he writes—

The world may be likened to a vast, as yet unordered garden, having diverse soils and aspects, some watered, some arid, some plain, some mountain; the different parts of which should properly be tended by different gardeners, having experience of diverse qualities of soil and aspect; but certain ones have seized upon the plots of others, and attempted to replace the plants natural to those plots, with others more acceptable or profitable to themselves. We have not to consider only the displaced gardeners, who naturally do not admire and are not grateful for the changes introduced into their plots; but to ask whether these proceedings are beneficial to the owner of the garden, for whom the gardeners work. Who are this owner but the Folk of the World of the future, which is ever becoming the present? (1981: 2–3)

Reiterating the other concerns of nationalism, Coomaraswamy says— 'Let us not forget that in setting this ideal of Nationalism before us, we are not merely striving for a right, but accepting a duty that is binding on us, that of self-realisation to the utmost for the sake of others' (1981: 4).

At this point, let us highlight the fact that Coomaraswamy's concern for others is different from the concern for others expressed by Western philosophers. For instance, Martha Nussbaum says, unlike Stoics who took good as 'interconnected in complex ways with that of others, taking the interlocking order of the entire world as the basic subject of deliberation', this attitude to politics is 'still too rare in the modern world. Even our major theories of justice—for example, that of John Rawls—take the nation as their basic unit, and say little about international justice or international concern' (1994: 507). She goes on to add in the footnote that—'This emerges clearly, for example, in some of the works of Michael Walzer (1983) and of Richard Rorty (1982). But international morality and justice are also little discussed in the work of some non-relativist thinkers who derive moral and political norms from historical traditions—e.g., Charles Taylor (1989)' (Taylor's current work addresses this gap).[2]

In contrast to this self-centred notion of nation, Coomaraswamy shows great concern for other societies. He suggests a wholly alternative model of development. In his model of nationalism, the nation strives not only for rights but also duties. In this model, industrial production 'can be organized on socialistic lines without converting the whole world into groups of state-owned factories'. Coomaraswamy adds—'It is for us to show that the great and lovely cities can be built again, and things of beauty made in them, without the pollution of the air by smoke or the poisoning of the river by chemicals; for us to show that man can be the master, not the slave of the mechanism he himself has created' (1981: 4).

Having set before the Indian nation the tasks assigned to it, Coomaraswamy goes on to identify the essential elements of the nation. 'Unity of some sort is essential', he writes, to make possible national self-consciousness, which contributes nationality. He points out how certain kinds of unity such as racial unity are not essential. However, there are two essentials of nationality and they are—a geographical unity, and a common historic evolution or culture. These two, he claims, 'India possesses superabundantly, besides many lesser unities which strengthen the historical tradition'. With regard to geographical unity, Coomaraswamy points out—

The fact of India's geographical unity is apparent on the map, and is never, I think, disputed.... The idea has been grasped more than once by individual rulers, — Asoka, Vikramāditya and Akbar. It was recognised before the Mahābhārata was written; when Yudhishtira performed Rājasuya sacrifice.... No one can say that any such idea as that of a Federated States of India is altogether foreign to the Indian mind.... Is it for nothing that India's sacred shrines are many and far apart; that one who would visit more than one or two of these must pass over hundreds of miles of Indian soil? (1981: 7–8)

Yet another source of this unity is in all the Indian schools of thought, in which, 'there runs like a golden thread the fundamental idealism of the Upanishads, the Vedānta, so in all Indian art there is a unity that underlies all its bewildering variety. This unifying principle is here also Idealism, and this must of necessity have been so, for the synthesis of Indian thought is one, not many' (1981: 17).

This unity in concrete form, Coomaraswamy reiterates, is as 'much for the advantage of others as of ourselves; and this without any feeling of bitterness or exclusiveness towards other races, though perhaps for a time such feelings may be inevitable' (1981: 13). It is not that this essential unity existed in abundance only in classical times; Coomaraswamy sees its continuity in contemporary times, particularly in the words of *Bande Mataram*, which, he explains 'are not the hysterical utterance of a people uncertain of their unity or doubtful of their future. They express the Indian recognition of the Motherland' (1981: 13).

There are two important arguments developed by Coomaraswamy's discussion of the nation. One is his attack on the outsider, and the other is his attempt to make out a case for *swaraj*. We will discuss these in some detail. First, Coomaraswamy refutes the allegation that the very idea of a national movement 'is the natural result of English education, and one of which England should in truth be proud, as showing that, under "civilisation" and the Pax Britannica, Indians are becoming, at last, capable of self-government'. Coomaraswamy claims that the 'facts are otherwise. If Indians are still capable of self-government, it is in spite of all the anti-national tendencies of a system of education that has ignored or despised almost every ideal informing the national culture' (1981: 96). He continues, 'as I have already indicated, the future lies not with the English educator in India, but with the Indian people and the National Movement. The responsibility of preserving and continuing the great ideals rests with these, and not with any foreign educator' (1981: 124).

In the context of combating the activities of Christian missionaries, he contrasts them with Buddhism and Hinduism, which, he states, 'are themselves missionary religions'. Preferring the example of Emperor Asoka (272 BC), who was a Buddhist, Coomaraswamy reminds us that he

> ... organized foreign missions on a truly magnificent scale. These were perhaps the most successful missions ever undertaken, for it was his support that "made the fortunes of Buddhism, and raised it to the position which enables it still to dispute with Christianity the first place among the religions of the world, so far as the number of believers is concerned" (Vincent Smith). With all his devotion to the Law of Buddha, what was his attitude to other sects? It is summed up in this extract from one of his edicts. "All sects have been reverenced by me with various forms of reverence. Nevertheless, personal adherence to a man's particular creed seems to me the chief thing." In another edict he says: "The adherents of the several sects must be informed that His Majesty cares not so much for donations or external reverence, as that there should be a growth, and a large growth, of the essence of the matter in all sects... The growth of the essence of the matter, assumes various forms, but the root of it is restraint of speech, to wit, a man must not do reverence to his own sect by disparaging that of another man for trivial reasons." What then was the burden of Asoka's missions, what was the message he so desired to communicate to all, what did he understand by conversion? It was not a dogma at all; it was the "Law of Piety" (*Dhamma*): "The Law of Piety is excellent. But what is the Law of Piety? It requires innocuousness, many good deeds, compassion, truthfulness, purity" (Pillar Edict II). This, with an insistence upon the greater value of meditation than of ceremonial observances, was the gospel of Asoka's missions. 'Conversion' was a turning of the heart, not the acceptance of a formula. Such was the work of the

greatest and most successful missionary the world has seen. Were the ideals of the Christian missionary similar, he might make fewer 'converts'—and more followers of Christ. (1981: 128–9)

There are two arguments attributed here to Asoka. One is reverence for others and the other is the importance of a change of heart as opposed to mere conversion. Coomaraswamy seems to be more preoccupied with the latter; with the result the former is not given proper attention. Rather, the first argument is a fact or a premise from which to derive the second one. I shall relate the second to the first argument later. Here, let me examine how Coomaraswamy subsequently generalizes Asoka's view of the larger category called India. Claiming religious tolerance for India, he writes—

In India any man may preach any doctrine even upon the temple doorstep. He may believe what he will, if only his practice do not undermine the structure of organized society. ["Hinduism has never produced an exclusive, dominant, orthodox sect, with a formula of faith to be professed or rejected under pain of damnation." (Vincent Smith, 'Asoka' p. 39.] There has never been a conflict between science and religion, for science has always been religious, and religion philosophical. It is a debated question whether there has ever been serious religious persecution in India; it is certain that it was the regular practice of Buddhist, Hindu, and some Muhammadan rulers, not merely to tolerate, but to support all sects alike. (1981: 130–1)

In addition to religious tolerance and the superior notion of a change of heart, Coomaraswamy claims that India possessed many other things before the arrival of colonialism (1981: 134–43). This included girls being educated in a 'highly specialised' way, in a form of education which was more 'culture than learning' (1981: 134). Refuting the claim that Hinduism contributed to Indian poverty by degrading the arts, Coomaraswamy writes that Sir George Birdwood should be allowed to respond to this ignorant and stupid statement. In the words of Birdwood—'In the happy religious organisation of Hindu village-life there is no man happier than the hereditary potter'. 'The Village communities have been the stronghold of the traditionary arts of India; and where these arts have passed out of the villages into the wide world beyond, the caste system of the Code of Manu has still been their best defense' (1981: 141).

When pointing out the religious discrimination faced by patients being treated in missionary hospitals, Coomaraswamy offers by contrast the example of King Duttha Gamani (161–137 BC), who, could say on his deathbed—'I have daily maintained at eighteen different places, (hospitals) provided with suitable diet, and medicines, prepared by medical practitioners for the infirm' (1981: 142).

Parakrama Bahu (AD 1164–1197) built a large hall that could contain many hundreds of sick persons (1981: 142). On the educational front, Coomaraswamy continues, 'Vijaya Bahu (AD 1236) established a school in every village' (1981: 143).

Refuting the allegations about India made by missionaries, Coomaraswamy refers to Sister Nivedita who had said that she had heard the following thirteen statements made and supported in a single speech—each statement has a familiar ring to the student of missionary literature. They were as follows—

1. That the Hindu social system makes a pretence of honouring women, but that this honour is more apparent than real.
2. That women in India are deliberately kept in ignorance.
3. That women in India have no place assigned to them in heaven, save through their husbands.
4. That no sacramental rite is performed over them with Vedic texts.
5. That certain absurd old misogynist verses … are representative of the attitude of Hindu men to their womenfolk in general.
6. That a girl at birth gets a sorry welcome.
7. That a mother's anxiety to bear sons is appalling; 'her wifehood depends on her doing so'.
8. That the infanticide of girls is a common practice in India.
9. That the Kulin Brahmin marriage system is a representative fact.
10. That parents unable to marry off their daughters are in the habit of marrying them to a god (making them prostitutes) as an alternative.

11. That Hindu wedding ceremonies are unspeakably gross.
12. That the Hindu widow lives a life of such misery and insult that burning to death may well have seemed preferable.
13. That the Hindu widow is almost always immoral.

Reacting to these he says—

> It would be waste of time to give the answers to these thirteen statements here; but I may, as Sister Nivedita does, classify them. Nos. 1, 3, 7, 11 and 13 are entirely false; Nos. 2, 5 and 12 are the result of misinterpreting or overstating facts; Nos. 4, 8, 9 and 10 may be true of certain limited localities, periods, or groups, yet are spoken of as representative of Hindu life as a whole. The last class is the most important; take only one example, No. 8; it is true that infanticide was at one time common amongst a certain class of Rajputs; but "it is in no sense a common Indian practice, any more than, if as much as, it is a common London practice." Indeed, in almost all these cases, a terrible *tu quoque* can be alleged,—not to speak of vices peculiar to the Christian West. (1981: 143–4)

Just observe how, without elaborating his refutation of these allegations, he suddenly retracts and says in the very next paragraph that 'I briefly review some other common missionary statements' (1981: 143–4). Defending the caste system he says—

> Of caste, only evil is spoken, its trade-guild and eugenic aspects being altogether ignored. It is related as horrible that men are divided into groups that may not intermarry; as if the situation were not almost identical in Europe, only there the rank depends more on wealth than on descent; and as if the missionary did not himself belong to the most arrogant of Indian castes, the Anglo-Indian. How many missionaries would care to see their daughters marry an Indian of any caste? (1981: 146)

Thus, there is an important difference between the nationalism of the West that rejects and dismantles the past, and the nationalism of India that, on the contrary, claims an imperative need to recall the past. And, Coomaraswamy made an immense contribution to this different version of Indian nationalism, which is an idealistic version. Through it, he and others made a case for swaraj. However, it is important to note that there are major differences between Coomaraswamy and other modern Indian philosophers, including Swami Vivekananda, Sri Aurobindo, and Mahatma Gandhi. In contrast to Coomaraswamy, these other Indian thinkers did not hold colonialism responsible for all of India's problems. Further, they also advocated internal, that is, self-criticism. The structural aspect of this was that their criticism of colonialism was always preceded by self-criticism (for more on this, see Raghuramaraju 2011). This move towards internal criticism in Vivekananda, Aurobindo, Rabindranth Tagore, and Gandhi was not available in Coomaraswamy's attempt at crafting an aesthetic nationalism. I am only pointing out the differences between these two groups of ideas. It is possible that Coomaraswamy did not agree with these thinkers and continued to advocate his own brand of nationalism. Before adjudicating the viability or even the desirability of each of these versions of nation, it is necessary to acknowledge the differences between the versions and classify them accordingly.

To return to Coomaraswamy's reference to Asoka, let me examine the historical precedence of universalism or internationalism that Coomaraswamy repeatedly lays claim to and attributes to Indian nationalism. A concern for other communities, and giving precedence to their welfare over one's own, are not attributes found in Hindu texts, in *Kautilya*, or *Manu*, or even in the two epics, all of which are clearly interested in the welfare of their own societies. Even the Advaitic idea of oneness is too abstract, and it does not operate at the societal level. The authors of these texts are essentially presenting strategies to combat other societies. However, concern for the other and for neighbouring societies is found in Emperor Asoka, the follower of Buddhism. Let me state this here.

Asoka, who renounced violence after the brutal Kalinga War, made a plea in his rock edicts for universal love, and following the path of Righteousness (Dharma—thirteenth rock edict). He reported how his own effort to follow this path culminated in making god mix with men, thus erasing the difference between great and small people. He wrote that one's parents and teachers should be obeyed, that pity should be felt for all creatures, including animals (first rock edict). According to Asoka, the king ought to love not only his own people but also those from beyond his frontiers. Asoka thus championed the welfare of the whole world. While recognizing cultural variability's between sects, he formulated fundamental common code to be followed by all—

> One should so control one's tongue as not to honour one's own sect, or disparage another's on the wrong occasions; for on certain occasions one should honour other men's sects. By doing this one strengthens one's own sect and helps the others, while by doing otherwise one harms one's sect and does a disservice to the others. Whoever honours his own sect and disparages another man's, whether from blind loyalty or with the intention of showing his own sect in a favourable light, does his own sect the greatest possible harm. (From the twelfth rock edict)

This idea of Asoka is closer to what is advocated by Coomaraswamy. It is interesting that though Coomaraswamy does refer to ideas drawn from Asoka in the passage quoted, he uses them to contrast Indian nationalism with Western nationalism. That is to say, Coomaraswamy merges the role of Buddhism into that of India as a whole, thus bringing in a distorting generality which defaces the unique contribution of Buddhism. While most of the contemporary Indian philosophers used the idea of internationalism associated with Indian freedom struggle, be it Swami Vivekananda, Sri Aurobindo, Mahatma Gandhi, and others, this facet has not figured in the academic discussions on the nation or Indian nation.

Here it may be noted that Coomaraswamy seems to be doing this because of his general thesis in another book where he denies differences between Hinduism and Buddhism.

There, he writes—'The more superficially one studies Buddhism, the more it seems to differ from the Brahmanism in which it originated; the more profound our study, the more difficult it becomes to distinguish Buddhism from Brahmanism, or to say in what respects, if any, Buddhism is really unorthodox' (1996: 45).

According to Coomaraswamy, the Buddha said—

'I have seen ... the ancient Way, the Old Road that was taken by the formerly All-Awakened, and that is the path I follow'; and since he elsewhere praises the Brahmans of old who remembered the Ancient Way that leads to Brahma, there can be no doubt that the Buddha is alluding to the ancient narrow path that stretches far away, whereby the contemplatives, knowers of Brahma, ascend, set free (*Vimuktah*), mentioned in verses that were already old when Yajnavalkya cites them in the earliest Upanishad. (1996: 46)

Reinforcing this continuity between Buddhism and Hinduism Coomaraswamy maintains—

If we can speak of the Buddha as a reformer at all it is only in the strictly etymological sense of the word: it is not to establish a new order but to restore an older form that the Buddha descended from heaven. Although his teaching is "all just so and infallible", this is because he has fully penetrated the Eternal law (*akalika dharma*) and personally verified all things in heaven or earth; he describes as a vile heresy the view that he is teaching a "philosophy of his own", thought out by himself. No true philosopher ever comes to destroy, but only to fulfil the Law. (1996: 45–6)

It is this absorption of Buddhism into Hinduism that prompts Coomaraswamy to juxtapose the idea of internationalism and the universalism that he advocates, with Indian nationalism. This is an ultimately problematic move. The philosophical problems that arise from the homogenization of Buddhism with Hinduism are explicated in the next chapter, which explores the views of Radhakrishnan, Ambedkar, and T. R. V. Murti on the relationship between Hinduism and Buddhism.

Notes

1. Recalling is different from reviving. For an interesting discussion on revivalism see Tapan Raychaudhuri (1989) and Amiya P. Sen (1993).
2. In addition to this nation-centredness of Western political theory, Western nation itself is not based on choice but is said to be driven by sociological determinism. Let us discuss this here. Accomplishing the ideals of the idea of nationalism involves, for Gellner, a

> ...general imposition of a high culture on society, where previously low cultures had taken up the lives of majority, and in some cases of the totality, of the population, ... It is the establishment of an anonymous, impersonal society, with mutually substitutable atomised individuals, held together above all by a shared culture of this kind, in place of a previous complex structure of local groups, sustained by folk cultures reproduced locally and idiosyncratically by the micro-groups themselves. This is what *really* happens. (1983: 57)

This nationalist project, it may be noted, is not philosophically defended but explained sociologically as a 'requirement of industrial society' and its 'cultural homogeneity', to which mankind is said to have been irreversibly committed. This paradigm of universal history, when confronted by the arguments of cross-cultural relativism, instead of answering the objections of the latter, explains them away by a sociologism according to which the agrarian plural society 'somehow or other' manage to overcome their particularities. Gellner, confronted by the argument of relativism, evades them by declaring—'The question concerning just *how* we manage to transcend relativism is interesting and difficult, and certainly will not be solved here.'

And asserts—'What is relevant, however, is that we somehow or other do manage to overcome it, that we are not helplessly imprisoned within a set of cultural cocoons and their norms, and that for some very obvious reasons ... we may expect fully industrial man to be even less enslaved to his local culture than was his agrarian predecessor' (1983: 120).

7

BUDDHISM IN INDIAN PHILOSOPHY

Radhakrishnan on Buddhism

Like Coomaraswamy, Radhakrishnan too tried to absorb Buddhism into Hinduism. He undertook this task in Volume I of his magnum opus, *Indian Philosophy*. Radhakrishnan expends a great deal of time upon accomplishing this task; he offers a variety of resources, and advances various philosophical arguments. To begin with, he does acknowledge the originality and uniqueness of the Buddha and Buddhism. With reference to early Buddhism he writes—

> There is no question that the system of early Buddhism is one of the most original which the history of philosophy presents. In its fundamental ideas and essential spirit it approximates remarkably to the advanced scientific thought of the nineteenth century. The modern pessimistic philosophy of Germany, that of Schopenhauer and Hartmann, is only a revised version of ancient Buddhism. It is sometimes said to be 'little more than Buddhism vulgarized.' As far as the dynamic conception of reality is concerned, Buddhism is a splendid prophecy of the creative evolution of Bergson. Early Buddhism suggests the outline of a philosophy suited to the practical wants to the present day and helpful in reconciling the conflict between faith and science. (2008: 287)

Therefore, in Radhakrishnan's assessment, Buddhism is original, it is a precursor—inspiring the pessimistic philosophy of Germany, it is practical and, more importantly, it is up-to-date. Having thus eulogized Buddhism, Radhakrishnan proceeds to identify certain important shifts in philosophy brought about by the Buddha, the most important being that while the Upanishads were 'a work of many minds', Buddhism on the other hand was 'considered creed of a single individual' (2008: 291). Indicating another difference between the Upanishads and Buddhism, Radhakrishnan states that in the 'Upanisads we have an amazing study of an atmosphere, in Buddhism the concrete embodiment of thought in the life of a man' (2008: 291). This shift away from many minds to a single individual and the ensuing unity of thought and life was, according to Radhakrishnan, what 'worked wonderfully on the world of the time' and was in fact responsible for the 'success of early Buddhism' (2008: 291).

Radhakrishnan proceeds to acknowledge Buddha's contribution. Buddha, he avers, 'wished to steer clear of profitless metaphysical discussions. Whatever metaphysics we have in Buddhism is not the original Dhamma but added to it (abhidhamma). Buddhism is essentially psychology, logic and ethics, and not metaphysics' (2008: 297). He first emphasized the special and novel aspects of Buddhism, noting the shift it brought about and acknowledging its contribution. This enhances the image of Buddhism. He, however, goes on to make his move to undermine the position of Buddhism. Let us see how he goes about this through a long chain of argumentation.

Radhakrishnan now reports that the Upanishads and Brahmanism's 'creed' was 'collapsing' and their system 'disintegrating'. The unsaid subtext of this statement by Radhakrishnan is that Buddhism did not take on a strong philosophical system but one that was already in decline. In this sense, the statement erodes the importance of Buddhism. Radhakrishnan goes on to explain, however, that it was against the background of this disintegrated system that Buddha sought to 'provide a firm foundation for morality' on the 'rock of facts' (2008: 300). This firm foundation provided by ancient Buddhism, claims Radhakrishnan, 'resembled positivism in its attempt to shift the centre from the worship of God to the service of man' (2008: 300–1).

Radhakrishnan then asserts that early Buddhism was 'not an absolutely original doctrine' (2008: 303). He reads the word 'original' to mean breaking away completely from the age and country— Radhakrishnan thus surprises the reader by claiming that Buddhism 'is no freak in the evolution of Indian thought' and 'Buddha did not break away completely from the spiritual ideas of his age and country' (2008: 303). As this statement shows, the definition of originality that Radhakrishnan uses is problematic; at the very least it is an interpolation within Buddhism, and is external to it. To substantiate his move, Radhakrishnan offers an argument by introducing a distinction; he writes—'open revolt against the conventional and legalistic religion of the time is one thing; to abandon the living spirit lying behind it is another' (2008: 303). There is something unconvincing about this change in Radhakrishnan's attitude towards Buddhism, but let us move on to analyse his next move. Claiming Buddha as part of a continuous ancient way of being, he declares that 'Buddha himself admits that the dharma which he has discovered by an effort of self-culture is the ancient way, the Aryan path, the eternal dharma' (2008: 303). Radhakrishnan writes—

> Buddha is not so much creating a new dharma as rediscovering an old norm. It is the venerable tradition that is being adapted to meet the special needs of the age. To develop his theory Buddha had only to rid the Upanisads of their inconsistent compromises with Vedic polytheism and religion, set aside the transcendental aspect as being indemonstrable to thought and unnecessary to morals, and emphasise the ethical universalism of the Upanisads. Early Buddhism, we venture to hazard a conjecture, is only a restatement of the thought of the Upanisads from a new standpoint. (2008: 303)

The reformist job done by Buddhism is pointed out once again, later in the book, when Radhakrishnan argues—

> In deducing the consequences of the Upanisad philosophy with incomparable beauty and logic, Buddha showed the inconsistencies in the beliefs and practices of those who paid lip allegiance to the Upanisads. While the bold speculators of the Upanisads adventured

on the naked peaks of the absolute, the masses of men were allowed to worship their little gods and perform the sacrificial ceremonies which they were supposed to demand. The elaborate sacrificial religion failed to command the confidence of the thoughtful in Buddha's time. (2008: 596)

Having denied Buddhism the status of a new dharma, Radhakrishnan concedes the following contributions made by Buddhism—(*a*) Buddha has rediscovered an old tradition; (*b*) he adopted this tradition in such a way so as to update it to meet the special needs of new and changed times; (*c*) in this context, Buddha rejected the inconsistencies in the Upanishads and set aside the transcendental aspects that are dispensable so far as morality is concerned.

In this view, Buddhism is not a break from tradition but a reformed, hermeneutic version of the same tradition. It is merely a new statement of an old tradition from a fresh standpoint. All the qualities that Radhakrishnan concedes to Buddhism lie within the general claim that it is not a new system but is a continuation of the existing one, *albeit* a reformed one. In other words, in Radhakrishnan's reckoning, reforming and repairing the decadent form of Brahmanism is the primary task of Buddhism. Thus, in his interpretation, Buddhism is largely parasitic on Brahmanism in need of reform, and possesses no autonomy of its own outside this ambit.

In support of his interpretation, Radhakrishnan quotes Rhys Davids, who holds a similar view of Buddhism. Based on this shared perspective, Radhakrishnan proposes to substantiate the claim that the 'spirit of the Upanisads is the life-spring of' early Buddhism (2008: 303–4). He does this by pointing out the aspects that these two philosophies have in common—

(*a*) Radhakrishnan claims that both the Upanishads and early Buddhism accept the 'doctrine of impermanence'. It is this doctrine that later forms of Buddhism developed into the concept of 'momentoriness' (2008: 313).

(*b*) He holds that the Buddha, 'following the Brahmanical theory, presents hell for the wicked and rebirth for the imperfect' (2008: 374).

(*c*) Radhakrishnan states that the 'only metaphysics that can justify Buddha's ethical discourse is the metaphysics underlying
the Upanisads'. He concludes from this that 'Buddhism is only
a later phase of the general movement of thought of which the
Upanisads were the earlier' (2008: 397).

To further substantiate his claims, Radhakrishnan also quotes
Max Müller who had held a similar view. Müller had written—'Many
of the doctrines of the Upanisads are no doubt pure Buddhism, or
rather Buddhism is on many points are consistent carrying out of
the principle laid down in the Upanisads' (Max Müller, S.B.E, XV;
Introduction, p. xxxviii) (in Radhakrishnan 2008: 397).

Radhakrishnan continues—'Buddha did not look upon himself
as an innovator, but only a restorer of the ancient way, i.e. the way
of the Upanisads. Both Buddhism and the Upanisads repudiate the
authority of the Vedas so far as their philosophy is concerned'
(2008: 397–8).

(*d*) Finally, he points out that the incomprehensibility of the absolute by the intellect is accepted by both the schools.

Thus, for Radhakrishnan, Buddhism '... is a return of Brāhmanism to its own fundamental principles. Buddha is not so much a
revolutionist who rode to success on the crest of the wave of reaction
against the Upanisad theory as a reformer whose aim was to remould
the prevalent theory of the Upanisads by bringing into prominence its
neglected truths' (2008: 398–9). Having drawn out the commonalities
between Buddhism and Brahmanism, Radhakrishnan states, however,
that Buddhism brought about the democratic practice of including
the masses by breaking open the exclusivism of the Upanishads. He
writes that Buddhism

> ...helped to democratise the philosophy of the Upanisads, which
> was till then confined to a select few. This process demanded that the
> deep philosophical truths which cannot be made clear to the masses
> of men should for practical purposes be ignored. It was Buddha's

mission to accept the idealism of the Upanisads at its best, and make it available for the daily needs of mankind. Historical Buddhism means the spread of the Upanisad doctrines among the peoples. It thus helped to create a heritage which is living to the present day. (2008: 398)

Nonetheless, even this concession to Buddhism that Radhakrishnan makes, in acknowledging its contribution towards democratizing Hinduism, is immediately undercut, when he goes on to say that such 'democratic upheavals are common features of Hindu history' (2008: 398). Revealing his desperation and the vulnerability of his position by resorting to examples from the post-Buddha period, Radhakrishnan writes that when 'the treasures of the great sages were the private property of a few, Rāmānuja, the great Vaisnava teacher, proclaimed the mystic texts to even the pariahs' (2008: 398).

Having underscored the attributes common to the two systems, Radhakrishnan makes the bold move of ironing out two major differences between Buddhism and Brahmanism, namely, the denial of *atman*, and the rejection of caste, by Buddha. With reference to the first, Radhakrishnan claims that Buddha advocated both *atma-vada* and *anatma-vada*—'The two doctrines were preached by Buddha for two very different objects. He taught the existence of Ātman when he wanted to impart to his hearers the conventional doctrine; he taught the doctrine of an-Ātman when he wanted to impart to them the transcendental doctrine' (2008: 328).

The Buddha's adherence to this dual position, according to Radhakrishnan, is played down by later interpreters like Nagasena, who 'drew the negative inference that there was no soul' (2008: 331). Nagasena, alleges Radhakrishnan, ignored Buddha's silence. By attributing the outright denial of atman, or at least a clear denial of it, to later interpreters like Nagasena, rather than to Buddha, Radhakrishnan bolsters his claim of continuity between Buddhism and Hinduism or more specifically, Buddhism's continuity with the Upanishads. Hence, according to Radhakrishnan, this difference between atman and *an-atman* is not a substantial one.

Making a further point, Radhakrishnan embarks on an explanation for yet another major difference between Hinduism and Buddhism, namely, the rejection of caste by Buddha. Radhakrishnan claims that Buddha does not 'oppose the institution [of caste], but adopts the Upanisad standpoint [which is that] [t]he Brāhmin or the leader of society is not so much a Brāhmin by birth as by character' (2008: 369). In Radhakrishnan's view, Buddha undermined that spirit of caste which later gave rise to inhuman practices.[1] Yet, even this reformist move, for Radhakrishnan, is not new to Brahmanical theory, as the latter too 'looked upon the highest status of the Sannyāsin as above caste' (2008: 370). Summing up his views on this topic he writes— '... in the world of thought both Upanisads and Buddhism protested against the rigours of caste. Both allowed the highest spiritual dignity to the poor and the humble, but neither rooted out the Vedic institutions and practices, though on this point Buddhism is a little more successful than Brāhmanism' (2008: 371).

Thus, for Radhakrishnan, Buddha did not reject caste outright as has been attributed to him; he only rejected its subsequent corrupt versions. More importantly, the Upanishads, in Radhakrishnan's interpretation, did not clearly advocate caste. As Radhakrishnan sees it, therefore, there is a nuanced view of caste, which is upheld by the Upanishads themselves, and this is merely reclaimed by Buddha, though with better success. Having identified all these common features between Buddhism and Brahmanism, Radhakrishnan makes yet another move in the same direction, and claims that Buddha is dependent on Hinduism. He writes—'The rules of Buddhist Sangha were borrowed from the Brāhmanical codes, though they were adapted to missionary purposes' (2008: 369).

At the end of the discussion, Radhakrishnan turns the matter on its head when he points out a central defect in Buddhism. He writes that the 'central defect of Buddha's teaching is that in his ethical earnestness he took up and magnified one half of the truth and made it look as if it were the whole' (2008: 399). Radhakrishnan attributes this error to Buddha's 'distaste for metaphysics' that consequently 'prevented him from seeing that the partial truth had a necessary complement and rested on principles which carried it beyond its self-imposed limits' (2008: 399). Explaining Hinduism's hostility towards Buddhism, Radhakrishnan, in a manner almost reminiscent of Foucault's criticism of Kant, which was alluded to previously, on the question of restricting freedom to the realm of thought and not extending it to the practical, writes—

> The Hindu quarrels not so much with the metaphysical conceptions of Buddha as with his practical programme. Freedom of thought and rigidity in practice have marked the Hindu from the beginning of his history. The Hindu will accept as orthodox the Sāmkhya and the Pūrva Mimāmsā systems of thought, regardless of their indifference to theism, but will reject Buddhism in spite of its strong ethical and spiritual note, for the simple reason that the former do not interfere with the social life and organisation, while the latter insists on bringing its doctrine near to the life of the people. (2008: 596)

Radhakrishnan goes on to add that 'while the Upanisads tolerated, even if they did not encourage the caste rules, Buddha's scheme definitely undermined the institution of caste' (2008: 597).

This is not only important but also interesting as it discloses the substantial threat Buddha poses to Brahmanism. While other schools of Indian philosophy offered differences in the realm of ideas, Buddhism threatened to intervene in social life and its organization. In this context, it sought to diminish the distance between theory and practice. It is this move by Buddha, according to Radhakrishnan, which threatened to change the organization of social life that incurred the wrath of the Hindus.

Thus, Radhakrishnan begins by acknowledging that Buddhism is original, modern, and scientific, a trend-setter, and a practical and updated school of thought. He then identifies Buddhism as a system that revolves around a single individual, and which sought to remove abstract metaphysics. Subsequently, as if reversing this view, Radhakrishnan claims that early Buddhism is not an original doctrine but merely presents the Upanishads from a new standpoint. In support of his assertion, Radhakrishnan points out common themes in

Buddhism and Hinduism, and explains the differences between the two, such as anatma-vada and the rejection of caste in Buddhism. While conceding that Buddhism broke open the exclusivist tendencies in the Upanishads, and facilitated the participation of the masses, Radhakrishnan nonetheless underplays this ostensibly unique characteristic too by claiming that these democratic overtures are also found in Hinduism, and thereby erasing this difference between Buddhism and Hinduism. In conclusion, Radhakrishnan points out the defects in Buddha's teachings and states the reasons for Hindus being intolerant of Buddhism. As I have already pointed out, there is something unconvincing about the long and arduous route of philosophical argumentation that Radhakrishnan has undertaken.[2] We must, however, note three points in his discussion—first, the politics of denying difference between Hinduism and Buddhism underlying his attempt; second, his solid and persistent attempt at offering a philosophical argument in support of his view; and finally, his acknowledgment of the sociological fact that Buddhism posed a real threat to Hindu society.

While disagreeing with Radhakrishnan's attempt to deny the differences between Buddhism and the Upanishads, we must, however, pay close attention to two other aspects. A close scrutiny of his argument shows that he is making two important points here—(*a*) he endorses Buddhism's attempt to reduce the gap between theory and practice present in corrupted versions of the Upanishads and Brahmanism; (*b*) he admits that this attempt by Buddha angered the Hindus.

Even though Radhakrishnan makes his point on behalf of Hindus, it must be noted that he concedes the fact that Buddhism did perform this act of attempting to reduce the gap. This fact was also highlighted by B. R. Ambedkar, although, unlike Radhakrishnan, he bolstered the radical difference between Buddhism and Hinduism. I will now discuss Ambedkar.

Ambedkar on Hinduism

In sharp contrast to both Coomaraswamy in the earlier chapter and Radhakrishnan in this chapter, there were many, including Ambedkar, who emphasized the radical stand of Buddha and Buddhism. Ambedkar rejected the Vedas and the Upanishads, and accepted Sankhya in addition to Buddhism in Indian philosophy. Interestingly, although he accepted Sankhya, he rejected the Bhagavad Gita. He claimed that the aim of the Gita was to 'defend certain dogmas of religion on philosophical grounds' (2010: 193). This is intriguing since the Gita is based on the metaphysics of Sankhya. Let me discuss Ambedkar's views on classical Indian philosophy.

For Ambedkar, the Vedas are a collection of mantras, i.e., hymns or chants, and are 'mere invocations to deities such as *Indra, Varuna, Agni, Soma, Isana, Prajapati, Bramha, Mahiddhi, Yama* and others'. There is not 'much philosophy in the Vedas' except 'speculations of a philosophical nature' about the 'origin' of the world, the creation of 'individual things', and their maintenance (2010: 205). Buddha, according to Ambedkar, 'did not regard all the Vedic sages as worthy of reverence,' but only 'ten Vedic Rishis'. He did not see anything 'morally elevating' in the Vedic mantras. Ambedkar argues that for Buddha, the '*Vedas* were as worthless as a desert', and so he 'discarded' them as 'useless' (2010: 207).

The Brahmanas are a part of the Vedas, and both are called *Sruti*. The Brahmanic philosophy, says Ambedkar, held Vedas as not only 'sacred' but also 'infallible'. Further, for Brahmanic philosophy 'performance of Vedic sacrifices and observances of religious rites and ceremonies and the offering of gifts to Brahmins' can save souls from transmigration and give them salvation. In addition to this, Ambedkar points out, Brahmins have a theory for an ideal society, that is, Chaturvarna, which entailed the division of the society into four classes—Brahmins, Kshatriyas, Vaishyas, and Sudras. These classes are not equal but are ruled by 'graded inequality'. The first one is placed at the top, while the last one is relegated to the bottom. There is also a division of occupations which is 'exclusive' and does not permit trespass. Another rule of this theory of an ideal society is that education must be denied to Sudras and women of all classes. A further rule is that a man's life is divided into four stages. This, Ambedkar explains, is the 'divine pattern of an ideal society called

Chaturvarna' (2010: 212). Finally, the Brahmanas also endorsed the doctrine of Karma (2010: 212).

The Buddha, insisted Ambedkar, 'strongly opposed' the thesis that the Vedas are 'infallible' and that their authority 'should never be questioned' (2010: 212). On the contrary, he declared that 'nothing was infallible and nothing could be final' (2010: 213). Buddha also denied any 'virtue in sacrifice'. While accepting sacrifice in the 'sense of self-denial for the good of others' as true sacrifice, the Buddha, regarded as false sacrifice the 'killing of animals as an offering to God for personal benefit' (2010: 213). He also rejected the theory of Chaturvarna as non-natural, arbitrary, rigid, and bereft of freedom. While conceding that inequality 'exists in every society', the Buddha, wrote Ambedkar, rejected Brahmanism that endorses graded inequality. Ambedkar explained—'Far from producing harmony, graded inequality, the Buddha thought, might produce in society an ascending scale of hatred and a descending scale of contempt, and might be a source of perpetual conflict' (2010: 214).

The Buddha found this ordering of the society to be not only selfish but also wrong, designed to serve the interests of a few at the cost of all, particularly, the Sudras and women. Being denied access to learning and education, these segments of the society did not know who was responsible for their degraded condition. Their ignorance, instead of making them rebel against Brahmanism, made them 'become the devotees and upholders of Brahmanism' (2010: 215). So, for these reasons, concludes Ambedkar, 'the Buddha rejected Brahmanism as being opposed to the true way of life' (2010: 215).

Let us now go on to discuss Ambedkar's critique of the Upanishads. According to Ambedkar, the '... main thesis of the *Upanishads* was that Brahman was a reality and that Atman was the same as Brahman. The Atman did not realize that it was Brahman because of the *Upadhis* in which it was entangled'. So, the question [as asked by the Upanishads] was—'Is Brahmana a reality?' In Ambedkar's reckoning, the 'acceptance of the Upanishadic thesis depended upon the answer to this question' (2010: 216). In contrast, says Ambedkar, the 'Buddha could find no proof in support of the thesis that Brahman was a reality. He therefore rejected the thesis of the *Upanishads'* (2010: 216). The question was put to no less a person than Yajnavalkya, 'a great seer who plays so important a part in the *Brihadarnyaka Upanishad'*. He was asked—'What is Brahman? What is Atman?' All that Yajnavalkya could say was—'*Neti*! *Neti*! I know not! I know not!' How can anything be a 'reality about which no one knows anything', asked the Buddha[3] (2010: 216). The Buddha had, therefore, no difficulty in rejecting the Upanishadic thesis as being based on pure imagination (2010: 216). In contrast to Radhakrishnan, Ambedkar saw no commonalities between the Upanishads and Buddhism. Rather, in Ambedkar's view, the Buddha clearly and wholly rejected not only the Vedas but also the Upanishads.

Though Ambedkar rejects outright the Vedas, Brahmanas, and the Upanishads, he accepts, together with Buddhism, the importance of one old system of Indian philosophy, that is, Sankhya. Ambedkar considers Kapila, the founder of Sankhya, to be the most pre-eminent 'among the ancient philosophers of India' (2010: 207). Ambedkar says of Kapila that his 'philosophical approach was unique' (Ibid.: 208), and the 'tenets of his philosophy were of a startling nature' (Ibid.), these qualities made him unique, so he stood 'in a class by himself' (Ibid.). Kapila insisted that 'Truth must be supported by proof'. He accepted only 'two means of proof', namely, 'perception' and 'inference'. While perception is defined as a 'mental apprehension of a present object', inference is 'threefold'. The three forms of inference are, writes Ambedkar—'(1) from cause to effect, as from the presence of clouds to rain; (2) from effect to cause, as from the swelling of the streams in the valleys to rain in the hills; and (3) by analogy, as when we infer from the fact that a man alters his place when he moves that the stars must also move, since they appear in different places' (2010: 207–8). The next tenet of Kapila's philosophy is related to 'causality—creation and its cause'. Resisting the obsession with knowing the creator of the universe, Kapila declared that 'a created thing really exists beforehand in its cause just as the clay serves to form a pot, or the threads go to form a piece of cloth' (2010: 208). There are, says Ambedkar, other grounds Kapila advanced in support of his rejection of the creator of the universe. According to Kapila, the

> ... non-existent cannot be the subject of an activity: There is no new creation. The product is really nothing else than the material of which it is composed: the product exists before its coming into being in the shape of its material of which it is composed. Only a definite product can be produced from such material; and only a specific material can yield a specific result. (2010: 208)

Instead, for Kapila, the

> ... empirical universe consists of things evolved (*Vyakta*) and things that are not evolved (*Avyakta*).... Individual things (Vyakta Vastu) cannot be the source of unevolved things (Avyakta Vastu).... Individual things are all limited in magnitude and this is incompatible with the nature of the source of the universe.... All individual things are analogous, one to another and, therefore, no one can be regarded as the final source of the other. Moreover, as they all come into being from a source, they cannot constitute that source. (2010: 208–9)

In keeping with the definition of causality, where 'effect must differ from its cause', Kapila claimed that the 'universe cannot itself be the final cause. It must be the product of some ultimate cause'. In response to the question why the 'unevolved cannot be perceived' Kapila said—

> It may be due to various causes. It may be that its fine nature makes it imperceptible, just as other things of whose existence there is no doubt, cannot be perceived; or because of their too great a distance or proximity; or through the intervention of a third object, or through admixture with similar matter; or through the presence of some more powerful sensation, or the blindness or other defect of the senses or the mind of the observer. (2010: 209)

In response to the question of the source of the universe, Kapila said that things 'that have evolved have a cause and the things that have not evolved have also a cause. But the source of both is uncaused and independent'. Explaining the process of evolution, he says that the 'process of development of the unevolved is through the activities of the three constituents of which it is made up, *Sattva*, *Rajas* and *Tamas*. These are called three *Gunas*' (2010: 209). Elucidating their nature he said—'The first of the constituents, or factors, corresponds to what we call as light in nature, which reveals, which causes pleasure to men; the second is that impels and moves, what produces activity; the third is what is heavy and puts under restraint, what produces the state of indifference or inactivity' (2010: 209).

Specifying the relations of the constituents with each other, Kapila said—

> The three constituents act essentially in close relation, they overpower and support one another and intermingle with one another. They are like the constituents of a lamp, the flame, the oil and wick.... When the three Gunas are in perfect balance, none overpowering the other, the universe appears (*achetana*) and ceases to evolve. ... When the three Gunas are not in balance, one overpowers the other, the universe becomes dynamic (*sachetan*) and evolution begins. (2010: 210)

Therefore, the presence of *duhkha* (suffering) is the reason for the Gunas to be in a state of imbalance, which causes disturbance. Of all the philosophers, writes Ambedkar, the Buddha was 'greatly impressed by the doctrines of Kapila' whose philosophy is based on 'logic and facts,' although the Buddha did not accept everything that Kapila taught. Specifying the three things Buddha accepted that came from Kapila, Ambedkar writes—'He accepted that reality must rest on proof. Thinking must be based on rationalism.... He accepted that there was no logical or factual basis for the presumption that God exists or that he created the universe.... He accepted that there was *dukha* (suffering) in the world...' (2010: 210).

The rest of Kapila's teachings, explains Ambedkar, the Buddha 'just bypassed as being irrelevant for his purpose' (Ibid.). The important point to note here is that Ambedkar's acceptance of Sankhya is related to the Buddha's acceptance of Kapila's system of philosophy.

An important dimension of Ambedkar's philosophy is that although he endorses the philosophy of Sankhya, he does not accept Bhagavad Gita which is based on the metaphysics of Sankhya. Also, Ambedkar made another interesting move, in this context, by revealing the close relationship between the Gita and Buddhism. That is, the treatment of the Gita in Ambedkar has to be seen in relation to both Sankhya and Buddhism. Let us then discuss Ambedkar's views on the Gita and its relation to Buddhism.

According to Ambedkar, the Gita is not a 'gospel', and hence it has 'no message'. It only defends 'certain dogmas of religion on philosophical grounds' (2010: 193). The first dogma the Gita defends is the justification of war on the basis of the mortality of human existence (2010: 194). Second, it defends the dogma of Chaturvarna by 'linking it to the theory of innate, inborn qualities in men' (2010: 194). The third such defence is of *Karma Marga*—that is, the selfish motive behind performance of the Karma is removed by 'introducing the principle of Anasakti, i.e., performance of Karma without any attachment for the fruits of the Karma' (2010: 195).

The dogmas which the Gita 'defends are the dogmas of counter-revolution as put forth in the Bible of counter-revolution, namely, Jaimini's *Purva Mimamsa*' (2010: 195). According to Ambedkar, the reason that it is 'necessary for the *Bhagvad Gita* to defend these dogmas' of 'counter-revolution' is to 'save them from the attack of Buddhism' (2010: 196). This is because the Buddha preached non-violence, a tenet which was accepted by most people in general, except the Brahmins. Under these conditions, brought about by the 'furious attack of Buddhism, Jaimini's counter-revolutionary dogmas were tottering and would have collapsed had they not received the support which the *Bhagvad Gita* gave them' (2010: 197).

Ambedkar dismisses the Gita's Chaturvarna theory. Referring to Krishna's defence of Chaturvarna, which is based on Sankhya's Guna theory, Ambedkar writes—'In the Chaturvarnya there are four Varnas. But the gunas according to Sankhya are only three. How can a system of four varnas be defended on the basis of a philosophy which does not recognize more than three varnas?' (2010: 197).

Underscoring the carefully timed efforts of the Gita to rescue the doctrines of counter-revolution, Ambedkar writes—'Nonetheless there is not the slightest doubt that without the help of the *Bhagvad Gita* the counter-revolution would have died out ... if the counter-revolution lives even today, it is entirely due to the plausibility of the philosophic defence which it receives from the *Bhagvad Gita* ...' (2010: 197–8).

Ambedkar goes on to claim that there is no difference between Jaimini's Purva Mimāmsā and the Bhagavad Gita. If there were any difference, it would lie, according to Ambedkar, in the Gita being a 'more formidable supporter of counter-revolution' and it's therefore providing a 'permanent basis which they never had before and without which they [that is the counter-revolutionaries] would never have survived' (2010: 198). In this context, Ambedkar asserts—contrary to those like Telang and Tilak—that the Gita 'has been composed after Jaimini's Purva Mimāmsā and after Buddhism' (2010: 199). Ambedkar rejects those 'typical' Hindu scholars who are 'reluctant to admit that the *Bhagvad Gita* is anyway influenced by Buddhism and is ever ready to deny that the *Gita* has borrowed anything from Buddhism' (2010: 202). With reference to these 'typical' Hindu scholars, Ambedkar writes—'It is the attitude of Professor Radhakrishnan and so also of Tilak. Where there is any similarity in thought between the *Bhagvad Gita* and Buddhism too strong and too close to be denied, the argument is that it is borrowed from the *Upanishads*. ..[to thus avoid] allow[ing] any credit to Buddhism on any account' (2010: 202).

Pointing out the similarities between the Gita and Buddhism, not only in 'ideas but also in language', he says—'The *Bhagvad Gita* discusses *Brahma-Nirvana*. The steps by which one reaches Brahma-Nirvana are stated by the *Bhagvad Gita* to be (1) *Shraddha* (faith in oneself); (2) *vyavasaya* (firm determination); (3) *Smriti* (remembrance of the goal); (4) *samadhi* (earnest contemplation) and (5) *prajna* (insight or true knowledge)' (2010: 203).

In identifying the source whence the Gita borrowed the Nirvana theory Ambedkar points out that as 'no *Upanishad* even mentions the word "Nirvana" the whole idea is peculiarly Buddhist and is

borrowed from Buddhism' (2010: 203). There are other ideas in the
Gita that are borrowed from Buddhism, Ambedkar asserts. They
are—the definition of a true devotee—'(1) *maitri* (loving kindness); (2) *karuna* (compassion); (3) *mudita* (sympathizing joy); and
(4) *upeksa* (unconcernedness)' (Ibid.). These are found in *Mahpadana
Sutta* and *Tevijja Sutta*. The other idea that the Gita takes from
Buddhism is on the question of what is knowledge, and what is ignorance. The explication, in chapter XIII, 'reproduced word for word
the main doctrines of Buddhism...' from the gospel of Buddha (2010:
204). Further, even the 'new metaphorical interpretation of karmas' in
chapter VIII is a 'verbatim reproduction of the words of Buddha' from
'Majjhina Nikaya I, 286 Sutta XVI' (2010: 203–4). Thus, Ambedkar
concludes that the

> ... *Bhagvad Gita* seems to be deliberately modelled on Buddhist
> *Suttas*. The Buddhist *Suttas* are dialogues. So is the *Bhagvad Gita*.
> Buddha's religion offered salvation to women and *Shudras*, Krishna
> also comes forward to offer salvation to women and *Shudras*.
> Buddhists say, 'I surrender to Buddha, to Dhamma and to Sangha.' So
> Krishna says, 'Give up all religions and surrender unto Me.' No paral-
> lel can be closer than what exists between Buddhism and the *Bhagvad
> Gita*. (2010: 204)

Therefore, we have in Ambedkar, an acceptance of Buddhism and
those aspects of Sankhya that were accepted by the Buddha, and a
complete rejection of the Vedas, Brahmanas, Upanishads, and the
Gita. The last, Ambedkar argues, is a response to Buddhism, and is
a philosophical defence of Purva Mimāmsā. While Radhakrishnan
denied any significant difference between Hinduism and Buddhism,
Ambedkar in contrast, reinforced the differences. While Ambedkar
uses the differences between Hinduism and Buddhism to claim
rejection of the former by the latter, Radhakrishnan, on the other
hand, explains the differences away to establish continuity between
the former and the latter. Yet, although Radhakrishnan attempts
to erase the differences between Hinduism and Buddhism—and
this may not be a politically correct thing to do—he seriously

engages with the issue and persistently pursues his line of argument, philosophically. For a similar position taken by Ranade, though at the level of social change, see Devare (2011). It is one thing to disagree with Radhakrishnan and another to dispense with him. Thus, there is a need to distinguish between political correctness and theoretical engagement. Not pursuing ideas with theoretical rigour can at times cost politics heavily. This is particularly so, not while making political claims, but when it comes to making sure political claims endure. In the case of Ambedkar, he is politically correct. He also engages with his contemporaries such as Telang, Tilak, and Radhakrishnan, and clearly states his disagreements with each of them. However, what Ambedkar has stated has not been progressively followed up and explored further by the philosophical community. Philosophers in India, while preoccupied with their ancestors and outsiders, did not in the first place recognize the possibilities made available by their predecessors. Relating philosophical dimensions to existing political debates is therefore an important, as well as an enormous, task.

So, there is a need to extend Ambedkar's engagement with different traditions and make these philosophically more rigorous, and to bring in rich resources from Buddhism, particularly in relation to Hinduism. In an interesting paper, Gopal Guru makes a claim for dalits to take to theory (2002). I would want to extend this, to include a philosophical engagement with Buddhism, and reopen the critical philosophical engagement with Hinduism. Along with the political claims clearly stated by Ambedkar, his philosophical insights and ideas available in his writings can be extensively elaborated.[4] These can be further related to the core, the fundamental philosophical themes in Buddhism as well as Hinduism. This opening between political ideas that are extended to philosophical discussions and insights that are formulated as philosophical theories; relating Ambedkar to Buddhism, and highlighting his critique of Hinduism; and reopening the critical relation between Buddhism and Hinduism—all these can reinvigorate the discussion on Indian philosophy. This kind of clearing of a space, or making an opening, has successful precedents, since this is what was undertaken by Buddhist philosophers in relation to the Buddha. They extended and philosophically formulated his ideas in a metaphysical discourse even though Buddha rejected metaphysics. The rich and extensive philosophical resources from Buddhism can be used to consolidate the critique of Hinduism initiated by Ambedkar. This, in my reading, would not only consolidate the political views that Ambedkar proposed, but also make the debate between Hinduism and Buddhism more current. Hence, we can say that Ambedkar brings political correctness to the discussion, making it more contemporary. However, one of the limitations in Ambedkar is that, in his preoccupation with exposing the injustice done by the Hindu society to dalits, he considers only the impact of Buddhism on the Gita, without considering the impact of Hinduism on Buddhism. In other words, both Radhakrishnan and Ambedkar tend to take extreme positions, albeit in opposite directions. It is in this context that I want to discuss the work of T. R. V. Murti.

Murti on the Mutual Interaction between Hinduism and Buddhism

Murti engages philosophically with Radhakrishnan's denial of differences between Hinduism and Buddhism. Like Ambedkar and Radhakrishnan, Murti credits Buddhism with offering a modern perspective. Murti takes a moderate position.[5] In his estimation, the 'egalitarian stand taken by Buddhism, as contrasted with the hierarchical pattern of Brāhmanism, in regard to the cultivation of spiritual life is in closer conformity with the ideals of today' (1983: 163). Directly taking on Radhakrishnan, he asks—'Does all Indian philosophy stem from one original source—the Upanisads? And are all Indian religions variations of the Vedic? Following the lead of Professor Radhakrishnan, the foremost Indian thinker of today, there is a large and impressive body of opinion favouring the unilinear tradition and development of Indian thought' (1983: 163).

Contesting this dominant view of unilinear development, Murti asserts that in the 'estimation of the Buddhist and non-Buddhist' that includes Jaina and Brāhmanical orthodox tradition, 'the differences between the two are radical'. Aside from these extreme positions, however, he claims that 'both these estimates seem to suffer from the fallacy of over-simplification. Probably the truth lies somewhere in the middle' (1983: 163). Specifying the nature of this middle path, Murti states that a 'careful analysis would reveal that Hinduism (Brāhmanism) and Buddhism belong to the same genus; they differ as species' (1983: 163–4). Using this formula, he goes on to emphasize a third dimension of the relation between Buddhism and Hinduism, namely, their complementary nature. This dimension eluded the attention of both Radhakrishnan and Ambedkar. Focusing on this complementary dimension, Murti clarifies—'In a sense, they are complementary to each other; one emphasises what the other lacks or slurs over. Without basic affinity they would have been completely sundered from each other ...' (1983: 164). And without differences they 'could not have vitalised and enriched each other. In view of the differences in their basic standpoints and the mode of their historical development, we should be alive to their differences as much as we affirm their affinities' (1983: 164).

Recounting the commonalities between them, Murti writes—

> Both Brāhmanism and Buddhism are types of spiritual religion. They try to realise a state of utter negation of the ego, the abolition of self-ishness. Positively, it is the attainment of the universal where all differences and conflicts cease and where there is concord and harmony. Again in both, the highest state is attained by a non-discursive intellectual intuition, a kind of mystic absorption .... Both religions have always believed in the Law of Karma as the Law of the Universe and as the arbiter of human destiny. (1983: 164)

Then, turning to the differences in their philosophies, he asserts—'All systems of Hindu thought subscribe to the *ātma-vāda* — the conception of reality as Being, substance and permanent. In its most radical form, as in the Vedānta of Sankara, it denied the reality of change, and characterised it as appearance' (1983: 164).

In contrast, writes Murti—

The Buddhist schools rejected the reality of the soul or substance (*anātmavāda*) and conceived the real as Becoming. The real for them is sequential, momentary, incessantly perishing and emerging …. Belief in the soul or the substance (*ātman*) is a basic wrong notion (Avidyā, ignorance) which is at the root of all suffering. Salvation would result if the belief in *ātman* is abandoned…. For the Vedānta, which may be considered as the most consistent form of Brāhmanical thought, ignorance is just the reverse; it is the conceiving of the real as changeful, different and particular. And when we realise the real as truly universal and identical (differenceless) as ātman, do we get freed of limitations and reach Brahmahood. (1983: 164–5)[6]

Besides these, there are other vital differences between the two systems with regard to their religious views. Underscoring these, Murti avers—

The religious differences are no less basic and striking. The source of religious inspiration in Brāhmanism is the revelation as given to us in the Vedas; in Buddhism it is reason. Not that Brāhmanism is antagonistic to reason or is unmindful of its value; but it is only revelation which can give us intuitions of the transcendent. The function of reason is to analyse and to clarify and, if necessary, to defend and to remove apparent contradictions …. The entire mode of development in Hinduism is authoritarian and traditional….

In contrast, to this, Buddha asks us not to receive anything on trust or to accept any authority, but to test it by reason and experience. He himself did not owe allegiance to any authority, Vedic or non-vedic. (1983: 165)

In further support of his statements, Murti writes in another work—

The opening dialogue of the *Digha Nikaya* (the *Brahmajāla Sutta*) indicates the standpoint of Buddha. He characterises all speculations as ditthi-vāda (dogmatism) and consistently refuses to be drawn into the net (jāla). He is conscious of the interminable nature of the conflict, and resolves it by rising to the higher standpoint of criticism. Dialectic was born. To Buddha, then belongs the honour of having discovered the dialectic long before anything approximating to it was formulated in the West. (2010: 40–1)[7]

The other irreconcilable difference between Buddhism and Hinduism, according to Murti is that—'For Buddhism the fundament is the moral consciousness and the spiritual urge is for purifying the mind of its passions (*visuddhi-mārga*). The fundament of Brahmanism is God-consciousness; and the goal is exaltation or deification' (1983: 166).

Thus, for Murti, the '*en rapport* relationship with God is what distinguishes Hinduism from Buddhism' (1983: 167). He states that 'the Mādhyamika, Vijnanavada and Vedanta exhibit some common features as to their form' but that 'they differ in the mode of their approach, and possibly with regard to that entity with which they identify the absolute' (1983: 171). Further, while the 'Vedanta analyses illusion from the knowledge-standpoint; the illusion consists in wrong characterisation, in mistaking the given as something else ...' the Vijnanavada, on the other hand, 'analyses illusion from an opposite angle; for it, the "given" is appearance, and the ideating consciousness alone is real' (1983: 173).

Rejecting those who, like Radhakrishnan, do not sufficiently emphasize these 'differences' and even tend to 'minimize' them, Murti declares—'It has been the fashion to consider that the differences between the Mādhyamika *sunyata* and *Brahman* are rather superficial and even verbal, and that the two systems of philosophy are almost identical. At least Professor Radhakrishnan thinks so, and Stcherbatsky's and Dasgupta's views are not very different' (1983: 177).

Reiterating his own position on this matter of the relationship between Hinduism and Buddhism, Murti says that 'although their generic identity is undeniable, the specific differences are equally undeniable' (1983: 219). Disagreeing further with Radhakrishnan, Murti claims that Buddhism's opposition to the Upanishads is not to be seen in Buddha's rejection of ritualism when the Upanishads themselves are wary of this practice, but rather in his rejection of atman. To quote—

> In the dialogues of Buddha we breathe a different atmosphere. There is a distinct spirit of opposition, if not one of hostility as well, to the ātmavada of the Upanisads. Buddha or Buddhism can be understood only as a revolt not merely against the cant and hollowness of ritualism—the Upanisads themselves voice this unmistakably—but against the ātma-ideology, the metaphysics of Substance-view. (2010: 16–17)

Refuting Radhakrishnan's claim that the Buddha was a follower of Upanishadic doctrine, Murti insists—

> Buddha nowhere acknowledges his indebtedness to the Upanisads or to any other teacher for his characteristic philosophical standpoint. Although Brahmā, the deity, is referred to several times, Brahman (the Absolute) is never mentioned. Buddha always considers himself as initiating a new tradition, as opening up a path never trod before. In the *Brahamajāla*, the *Samaññaphala Sutta* and elsewhere, current philosophical speculations are reviewed; and all of them are rejected as dogmatic (ditthivāda) and as inconsistent with spiritual life. This is not the way of one who continues an older tradition. It is not correct to hold that the differences are religious and practical, although they are put up as philosophical. (2010: 17)

Trenchantly questioning Radhakrishnan's interpretation of the Buddha's silence with regard to atman, Murti writes—

> If the ātman had been a cardinal doctrine with Buddhism, why was it so securely hidden under a bushel that even the immediate followers of the Master had no inkling of it? The Upanisads, on the other hand, blazen forth the reality of the ātman in every page, in every line almost. Buddha came to deny the soul, a permanent substantial entity, precisely because he took his stand on the reality of moral consciousness and the efficacy of Karma. (2010: 17)

To support his analysis, Murti elucidates the implications of accepting atman for its spiritualism and moral dimension. He says—

> An unchanging eternal soul, as impervious to change, would render spiritual life lose all meaning; we would, in that case, be neither the better nor the worse for our efforts. This might lead to inaction (akriyāvāda). Nay more; the ātman is the root-cause of all attachment, desire, aversion, and pain. When we take anything as a self (substantial and permanent), we become attached to it and dislike other things that are opposed to it. Sakkāyaditthi (substance-view) is avidyā (ignorance) *par excellence*, and from it proceed all passions. Denial of Satkāya (atman or Substance) is the very pivot of the Buddhist metaphysics and doctrine of salvation. (2010: 17)

Having identified the genus-like similarities and species-like differences, Murti then highlights the active and negotiated relations between the two schools of thought. Murti's contribution lies in elucidating this transformative relation between Hinduism and Buddhism, rather than merely stating either differences or absence of differences. This is what distinguishes Murti from both Ambedkar and Radhakrishnan. Ambedkar recognizes only the impact of Buddhism on the Gita and does not see any significant influence of Hinduism on the shaping of Buddhism. While Radhakrishnan sporadically, strategically, and infrequently acknowledges the interrelations between the two systems, in the end, he underplays them by subsuming Buddhism within Brahmanism, thus making the process of transformation restricted and less significant. In Radhakrishnan, it becomes a marginal activity overshadowed by his overall concern, which is to correct Brahmanism through the critical application of Buddhism. In contrast, Murti claims that—'There has been considerable research on the influence of Buddhism on the Brāhmanical systems of thought and *vice-versa* …. Here too a balanced view may be considered as possibly nearer the case' (1983: 168).

Stating in clearer terms the nature of influence, Murti writes that influence can be 'expressed as much through opposition as by acceptance' (1983: 168). Two ideas can thus influence each other both negatively and positively. Accounting for the transformation within Buddhism, Murti asserts that in its earlier phase it 'was a radical pluralism [subsequently has become] in the Mahāyāna a radical absolutism with a different conception of Buddha and the Bodhisatva ideal' (1983: 168). He attributes this transmutation to two factors, one internal and the other external. These are—

> … one that of borrowing from or being influenced by the Upanisadic thought where absolutism and theism are such dominant features; the other hypothesis would deny external influence and see the account for the revolution as the result of an inner dynamism in Buddhist thought itself. These two views are not exclusive, and perhaps the truth lies somewhere between the two. (1983: 169)

The first view, according to which the 'Upanisadic Brahman is obviously the model from which the *Tathatā* or *sūnyatā* has been drawn. Competent scholars, like Kern, Keith, Stcherbatsky and Radhakrishnan among others, have drawn pointed attention to the probable influence of the Upanisadic thought on the emergence of the Mahāyanā' (1983: 169). Murti, on the other hand, gives more importance to the second view. He writes, 'I attach somewhat greater importance to the dynamism inherent in Buddhism itself which engendered the revolutionary change' (1983: 169). While holding internal reasons responsible for the changes in Buddhism, Murti does not wholly discount the influence of external reasons. Pointing out another example of influence of the Upanishads on Buddhism, he says—

> The dialogues of Buddha, as preserved in the Pāli Canons, are suggestive; they are as little systematic as the Upanisadic texts. Buddhist systems grew out of them much in the way the Brāhmanical systems grew out of the Upanisads. Buddhism is a matrix of systems, and not one unitary system. It does not exclude legitimately different formulations. For a correct and fruitful understanding of the development of Indian philosophy, it is necessary to admit not only the difference between Buddhist and Brāhmanical systems of thought, but also internal differences within Buddhism itself. This would be evident if we

consider the nature and development of the Upanisadic and Buddhist thought. (2010: 14–5)

Later in the same work he claims—'There were lively interchanges between the Buddhist and the Brāhmanical logicians for centuries. The Mādhyamika and Aupanisada schools were not enclosed in water-tight compartments' (2010: 113).

After elucidating the influence of the Upanishads in systematizing Buddhism, Murti turns his attention to highlighting the influence of Buddhism on subsequent philosophical activity in India. With regard to Advaita, an influential school of Hindu philosophy, Murti propounds—

> The development of the Advaita Vedānta offers us a close parallel on the ātma tradition. The Upanisads affirm Brahman (Absolute Spirit) as the sole reality of the world. The Upanisadic seers reach this absolutism not so much through reasoning as by inspiration. They are more suggestive than systematic. The Advaitism (Non-dualism) of Sankara is established on a dialectical basis by the criticism of the Sānkhya, the older Vedānta and other systems. For its dialectical technique the Vedānta is clearly indebted to the Mādhyamika. (2010: 9)

Thus, Buddhism has drawn from the Upanishads for its methodology of systematizing the dialogues of the Buddha, and Advaita has incorporated the Buddhist dialectical technique. And Vedānta, writes Murti,

> ... profited by the technique or method of the Mādhyamika. [Vedantin] had before him the Mādhyamika distinction of paramārtha and samvrti, of texts into nitārtha and neyārtha, his reaching the real by the method of negating the unreal appearance etc. The Mādhyamika and Yogācāra also had a theory of illusion to account for the emergence of appearance. Knowledge of this turn in Buddhism must have sent the Vedāntin back to his own texts and enabled him to perceive the truer meaning of the Upanisads in advaitism. Presumably, there has been borrowing of technique and not of tenets. (2010: 116–17)

Recounting yet another, subsequent, instance of the transformative relations between Buddhism and Hinduism, Murti points out— 'Gaudapāda appears to us as the Brāhmanical thinker boldly reformulating the Upanisadic ideal in the light of the Mādhyamika and Vijñānavāda dialectic. But there was more borrowing of technique than of tenets' (2010: 13).

Similarly, there is borrowing of method from Buddhism. Murti observes—

> Sri Harsa, as is well known, employs the Mādhyamika method in his *Khandana Kanda Khādya* and even says so in so many words. Our explanation of similarity of method and technique accounts for the accusation by Bhāskara and other non-advaita Vedāntins against Sankara and his followers as introducing Mahāyanikā-naya (pravesa) and as being Buddhists in disguise (prachanna-bauddhas); it at once preserves the doctrinal originality of the Vedānta. (2010: 117)

The important point in Murti's argument is the dialectical relation between Hinduism and Buddhism.[8] However, while there are many political dimensions to Murti's critique of Radhakrishnan, which are close to Ambedkar's analysis, Murti either does not perceive these or stops short of relating his work to them.

Thus, we have in Radhakrishnan, a philosophical engagement wherein his attempt to claim Buddhism as part of Hinduism, he denies or explains away, though less than convincingly, the differences between Buddhism and Hinduism. Radhakrishnan does however concede, though only in passing, the fact that Buddhism threatened to change the social system of Hindus, and he leaves it at that. Subsequently, we have in Ambedkar a different effort, in sharp contrast to Radhakrishnan, wherein he highlights the differences between Hinduism and Buddhism, and claims the Buddha as being outside the Hindu fold. Murti takes a moderate position, keeps the discussion at a philosophical level, and challenges Radhakrishnan on many counts.

The transformative aspect of the associations between Hinduism and Buddhism that Murti emphasizes can be extended to understand the relationship between the modern and the pre-modern in India.[9]

While denying the difference to project unity and cultural continuity as a defence against colonialism may be understandable, the manner in which the denial is executed may not be justified. What Independent India requires is not mere unity or mere difference, nor even unity in diversity. We need to go much beyond these.

There is a need to identify and nurture the differences that are available. There is a further need to debate these differences on reasonably objective and common grounds. Arguments are one aspect of a debate. In a debate the participants only claim what is truth. What is truth is adjudicated not by the participants but an outsider. An outsider could be an expert or as in democracy it could be the common person. So what is suggested here is not mere identification of difference as was the preoccupation of the orientalists; nor expressing ideas in isolation; not even dialogue between two cultures or schools of thought which largely remains less rigorous; not mere arguments, but rigorous and relentless debates. Modern India provides several complex debates for philosophy to rejuvenate itself.

Notes

1. Making a similar point Coomaraswamy says that

> ... the Brahmans of today—although there are exceptions—have fallen from the graces that pertained to their pure and selfless ancestors. It is from this point of view, and in connection with the fact that Buddha is born in an age when the royal caste is more than the priestly caste in honour, that we can best understand the reason of the promulgation of the Upanisads and Buddhism at one and the same time. These closely related and concordant bodies of doctrine, both of 'forest' origin, are not opposed to one another, but to a common enemy. The intention is clearly to restore the truth of an ancient doctrine. Not that the continuity of transmission in the lineages of the forest hermitages had ever been interrupted, but that the Brahmans at court and in the world, preoccupied with the outward forms of the ritual and perhaps too much concerned for their emoluments, had now become rather, 'Brahmans by birth' (*brahmabandhu*) than Brahmans in the sense of the Upanishads and Buddhism, 'knowers of Brahma' (*brahmavit*). There can be little doubt that the profound

doctrine of the Self had hitherto been taught only in pupillary succession (*guruparampara*) to qualified disciples; there is plenty of evidence for this on the one hand in the Upanishads themselves (the word itself implies 'sitting close to' a teacher) and on the other hand in the fact that the Buddha often speaks of 'holding nothing back'. The net result of these conditions would be that those to whom the Buddha so often refers as the 'uninstructed multitude' must have entertained those mistaken 'soul theories' and beliefs in the reincarnation of the 'personality' against which the Buddha fulminates untiringly. (1996: 47)

2. It is possible to argue that Radhakrishnan seems to be denying differences between these two systems not so much because he—or even Coomaraswamy—was instituting new politics but extending the politics of the indologists such as Max Muller, Rhys Davids, whose work they cite in support. Further, Radhakrishnan's exercise in these two volumes of *Indian Philosophy* may be seen more as dismantling the organic interaction, even though disintegrated, systems, and pack them to be transported to a new and alien habitation, like the textbooks, bereft of the interactions. He seems to be pushing these diverse interactive systems into a small suitcase. Taking off from this, we can unpack what was packed by those like Radhakrishnan, reorganize them in a new space, highlight not only the dynamic relation between these Indian philosophical schools but also use this idea to understand the new modern social relations that came to India with the advent of colonialism. Lal Mani Joshi (1983), in the context of discussing the Brāhmanical School's attempt at viewing Buddhism 'as a form or branch of Hinduism' (1983: 8) initiated by those like Swami Vivekananda, briefly and sporadically discusses Radhakrishnan's similar attempt. Joshi while criticizing this tends to see this also perhaps as a 'demand of dynamics of national reform' (1983: xxi).

3. Vivekananda, Krishna Chandra Bhattacharyya, and R. D. Ranade take up for elaborate discussion the issue concerning the idea of ultimate reality in the Upanishads. For instance, distinguishing the sense of unknowability in Kant and Spencer, Ranade claims that the unknowability in the Upanishads is to be understood from the 'standpoint of philosophic humility' (in Bhushan and Garfield 2011: 263).

4. In my 2009, I have explicated the underlying philosophical reasons behind Ambedkar's decision to embrace Buddhism. To see the political reason, I have argued that there is an underlying philosophical

preference though not explicitly claimed and argued that must be identified. This in my view is the following. Ambedkar is against caste, which is a breeding ground for the social evil, untouchability. Caste is one of the aspects of hierarchy. Hierarchy can grow only on permanence. Buddhism does not accept permanence, but change. If everything is changing and nothing is permanent, then hierarchy cannot be sustained. In turn, without hierarchy, caste cannot survive. This is the deeper and underlying philosophical reason behind Ambedkar's decision to embrace Buddhism. In my other work, 2011, I have analysed the difference between Descartes's decision to leave tradition and embrace modernity simultaneously and Ambedkar taking nearly twenty-seven years between his decision to leave Hinduism and convert to Buddhism.

5. To complain about Radhakrishnan's work as Satchidananda Murty does in the earlier chapter is one thing but to engage with him is another. Murty, however, does not refer to T. R. V. Murti's criticism of Radhakrishnan.

6. Distinguishing these two models of philosophy he says—

> There are two main currents of Indian philosophy—one having its source in the ātma-doctrine of the Upanisads and the other in the anātma-doctrine of Buddha. They conceive reality on two distinct and exclusive patterns. The Upanisads and the systems following Brāhmanical tradition conceive reality on the pattern of an inner core or soul (ātman), immutable and identical amidst an outer region of impermanence and change, to which it is unrelated or but loosely related. This may be termed Substance-view of reality (atma-vāda)....
>
> The other tradition is represented by the Buddhist denial of substance (ātman) and all that it implies. There is no inner and immutable core in things; everything is in flux. Existence for the Buddhist is momentary (ksanika), unique, (svalaksana) and unitary (dharmamātra). It is discontinuous, discrete and devoid of complexity. The substance (the universal and the identical) was rejected as illusory; it was but a thought-construction made under the influence of wrong belief (avidyā). This may be taken as the *Modal view of reality*. (2010: 10–11)

7. After discussing various aspects of Hinduism and Buddhism in this later book, he says—

> We are now in a position correctly to indicate the relation between the Upanisads and Buddha. Both have the same problem, Pain (duhkha), and they see it in all its intensity and universality, Phenomenal existence is imperfection and pain. Both again are one in placing before us the ideal of

a state beyond all possibility of pain and bondage. The Upanisads speak of it more positively as a state of consciousness and bliss (vijñānam ānandam brahma). Buddha emphasises the negative aspect of it: Nirvana is the annihilation of sorrow. Both have to speak of the ultimate as devoid of empirical determinations, as incomparable to anything we know; silence is their most proper language. They also agree that no empirical means, organisational device, sacrifice or penance, can bring us to the goal. Only insight into the nature of the real can avail. For the Upanisads, the atman is real; only its identification with the body (kosas), the states or any empirical object, is accidental. By negating the wrong identification, its unreal limitations, we can know its real nature. Ātman is Brahman; there is no other to it. No fears, aversion or attachment could afflict it. To realise the self (ātmakāma) is to have all desires satisfied (āptakāma), and thus to transcend all desires (akāma).

Buddha reaches this very goal of desirelessness, not by the universalism of the I (ātman), but by denying it altogether. For, only when we consider anything as permanent and pleasant, as a self, do we get attached to it and are averse to other things that are opposed to it; there is then bondage (samsāra). (2010: 18–19)

8. This aspect is also found in the work of D. R. Nagaraj who also elaborates the mutual transformation of Ambedkar and Gandhi (1993).
9. While distinguishing Murti's account from Radhakrishnan, I am aware of the fact that there are those like N. S. S. Raman who while recognizing Murti's 'profound scholarship in both traditions of Buddhism and also in the various systems of Indian philosophy', however reminds that Murti's 'judgment nevertheless is influenced by his transcendentalist approach, not dissimilar to the Advaitic world view' (1989: 80). Raman while drawing close similarities between Radhakrishnan who is an *Advaitin* and Murti classifies the latter as a 'Hindu Buddhist' as alleged by Sri Lankan scholars about some Indian Buddhists.

CONCLUSION

There is a close and distinctive relationship between philosophy and India. Philosophy is not just another subject but a foundational one. It is this status of philosophy that Krishna Chandra Bhattacharyya had in mind when he claimed that it is in 'philosophy, if anywhere' that the task of 'discovering the soul of India is imperative for modern India'. This is the civilizational task before philosophy in India, but even if one takes a sympathetic view of the practice and activities of the subject in this country, its current status comes nowhere near the expectations of Krishna Chandra Bhattacharyya.

Particularly over the last century, India had started to become an important site offering different forms of development. Unlike in the West, where the pre-modern is quarantined and modernity is accepted and inhabited, in India, modernity must co-exist with the pre-modern. Defying the liberal canon, which makes literacy the prerequisite for sustaining democracy, Indian democracy is sustained mostly by those who are not literate. More specifically, in contrast to the West, where disinheriting the past is a prerequisite to forming a nation, in India, invoking the past is the invariable undertaking aspect of all modern Indian philosophers, including Ambedkar, who reinstated both Buddhism and Sankhya by making a complex distinction between Sankhya and the Gita. Dissociating the Gita from Sankhya philosophy, whose metaphysics the text borrows, is as problematic as Gandhi interpreting the Gita as a text of non-violence when it clearly endorses violence and war. Leaving aside the obvious politics associated with these views, what is important, in my view, is that unlike the modern Western philosophers, recent Indian philosophers have reiterated—though there is a great deal of variability in the content of their reiterations—their ancestors. Let us examine how one of them, Sri Aurobindo, takes stock of the situation in his time, recalls the past, and negotiates with outsiders. While rejecting the hierarchy between the rulers from outside and India as the ruled, Aurobindo establishes a commonality between the two, not in their achievements, but in their mistakes. He writes—

> We have both made mistakes, faltered in the true application of our ideals, been misled into unhealthy exaggerations. Europe has understood the lesson, she is striving to correct herself; but she does not for this reason forswear science, democracy, progress, but purposes to complete and perfect them, to use them better, to give them a sounder direction. She is admitting the light of the East, but on the basis of her own way of thinking and living, opening herself to truth of the spirit, but not abandoning her own truth of life and science and social ideals. We should be as faithful, as free in our dealings with the Indian spirit and modern influences; correct what went wrong with us; apply our spirituality on broader and freer lines, be if possible not less but more spiritual than were our forefathers; admit Western science, reason, progressiveness, the essential modern ideas, but on the basis of our own way of life and assimilated to our spiritual aim and ideal; open ourselves to the throb of life, the pragmatic activity, the great modern endeavour, but not therefore abandon our fundamental view of God and man and nature. There is no real quarrel between them; for rather these two things need each other to fill themselves in, to discover all their own implications, to awaken to their own richest and completest significances. (in Bhushan and Garfield 2011: 63–4)

The barter that Aurobindo is offering, for all that it is not taken seriously by the other side, is nonetheless worth analysing. What are the components of the transaction? Does this transaction amount to adding the strength of one civilization with another civilization? That is, making one plus one into two. Or is it adding two halves and making into one. This is a serious issue that needs to be discussed in detail.

India is different from the West, although not in the way projected by the Orientalists who plot the difference along the materialism-and-spiritualism axis. India is different in offering different combinations of matter and spirit, change and permanence, unity and diversity. All cities in India, except for Chandigarh, are extensions of a village or villages. This fact poses other problems of legitimacy, in terms of the rural and the urban co-existing with each other. What are they doing with each other? Are they unrelated to each other? Are the cities encroaching into the villages, making them victims—the wretched of the earth? Yet, at the same time, are not the villages frustrating the cities? Is not each surreptitiously seeping into the other at different levels, like water seeping into black cotton soil? Or, is it the case, that while the city floods the village, the village in turn slowly dampens the city? While motor vehicles forced the villages to move faster, villages, on the other hand, too seem to be forcing sports vehicles on the road to learn how to walk during traffic jams. The variabilities that are available in Indian society today, and the fact that 'it is the most interesting country' (Ramachandra Guha 2008: 193) are not achievements by themselves. They can, however, be turned into them, if one starts working on doing this seriously and judiciously. What we have before us today is a mere difference. This has to be transformed to become distinct, and, in turn, become unique. Making this transformation requires having competence, keeping in mind a larger global perspective alongside attending to the details. To begin with, we must ask—*if* Indian democracy is sustained mainly by non-literates, where does this extraordinary capability or virtue come from? Does it arise from modernity or from the pre-modern, or is it in the use of the modern by the pre-modern? Or might it be the failure of the modern on the one hand, but the success of the pre-modern on the other? Further, if this Indian instance, of a democracy upheld by non-literate citizens, is true, then does this make literacy not a necessary but a merely contingent prerequisite for sustaining democracy? If the relation is contingent then it goes against the canon set by liberals for democracy. One needs to initiate a long-drawn out process to convert differences into virtues lest they should remain merely, as *de facto*, or, worse, disappear with changing times.

Unfortunately, academic philosophy in India has not been able to respond satisfactorily to the wonderful and novel combinations of systems and ideas available in India. One of the reasons why this is so is that philosophers are preoccupied with their ancestors, whose relationship with the present has been disrupted by the arrival of colonialism and modernity. Their preoccupation of present-day philosophers with outsiders remains as half-hearted as their attempt to transplant new ideas and theories from the West, which has met with varying degrees of success. Thus, they are far removed from both their ancestors and outsiders. Despite some sporadic efforts that are creative and innovative to practice philosophy in India, the results have not been promising. This, to my mind, is not because Indian society and its culture are becoming ever more uninteresting, or because of a lack of current talent. In my analysis, it is because we are refusing to admit the disruption that creates the gap between present-day philosophers and their ancestors or outsiders. (Ramachandra Guha alluded to another kind of gap in Indian history, which he claimed, was largely preoccupied with the British and with colonial history and has neglected the post-Independence history of India [see Guha 2008]). In addition, we are failing to take into consideration the efforts and the work of our predecessors who tried strenuously and consistently to deal simultaneously with both ancestors and outsiders. These predecessors' works need not be taken as final, but they can provide a good bridge in the interim to establish a relationship between the ancestors and outsiders.

In order to prepare a firmer ground for philosophy in India it is necessary to rejuvenate academic philosophy. In this work, I have suggested that this can be done by critically evaluating the contributions of some of the academic philosophers in India. The first part of the book has shown how both Krishna Chandra Bhattacharyya and Bilgrami failed to take into account the use of the resources of their predecessors to solve the problems of those from the modern West;

examples include Thomas Aquinas, Socrates, and Jesus Christ. I have also discussed in this part, Matilal, who offers an epic as a source to obtain ethics. In the second part, I have pointed out how Daya Krishna and Satchidananda Murty did not take into consideration the philosophical contributions of Swami Vivekananda, Sri Aurobindo, Mahatma Gandhi, and others. The final part demonstrated how to critique contemporary attempts by both Coomaraswamy and Radhakrishnan that deny differences between Hinduism and Buddhism. In this context, the last chapter draws into the discussion philosophically significant individuals like Ambedkar and Murti both at a philosophical and political level. I hope that this evaluation of some of the modern philosophers of India gives a clear picture about both some of our achievements as well as some of our limitations.

Here, it is necessary to acknowledge that the predecessors I have referred to are not systematic philosophers, but more like writers. Pre-modern society in India had continuously made attempts to transform these writers into traditional icons, such as the Mahatma, the Swami, Yogi, Gurudev, and so on. However, modern institutions, particularly educational institutions, have not succeeded in converting these writers into authors.

Aurobindo may be a good writer, but he is not necessarily a consistent author. This is true of other writers of this period, such as Vivekananda, Gandhi, and Ambedkar. But independent India needs authors as well as texts. We do not have the readymade resources of authors or even the 'founders of discursivity' a la Foucault (1994: 350). We also do not have many of what Raymond Williams calls 'indicative' or 'subjunctive' texts (1986: 16). Our writers are more like 'antiseptic' and 'disinfected' interlocutors, to use Edward Said's characterization (1989: 210). Here, it is relevant to briefly refer to V. S. Naipaul. While discussing Gandhi's *Hind Swaraj*, he wrote that the 'book would not be read in India, not even by scholars (and still hasn't been), but its name would often be taken as a milestone in the independence struggle, and it would be cherished as a holy object' (2008: 166–7). Thus, there is a cultural tendency in India to turn writings into holy objects, and the thinkers and writers of these texts into

gurus, mahatmas, swamis, and saints. This activity, carried over from
the pre-modern period, will continue. At the same time, it is necessary to present the modern Indian philosophers in a systematic and
formal way, keeping in mind that situations change.

Therefore, there is a need to convert these writers into authors,
and their writings into texts. This can be done by bringing in for-
malism, by making larger comparisons, and by identifying striking
differences. For instance, this is what has been done by Bilgrami
with regard to Gandhi (2006), J. L. Mehta for Krishna Chandra
Bhattacharyya (1974), and Ramchandra Gandhi for Mahatma Gandhi
with regard to the earthquake in Bihar (1983). This is the job that
post-independence academic institutions in India, including universities, could have undertaken. But work in this direction is sporadic and
often unsatisfactory. It is against this dim background that philosophy
in India has to now seriously recognize and incorporate within itself
the contribution of its predecessors both in the West and in India,
and, in this way, prepare the ground for a philosophy to theorize
India, which *is* a wonder.

GLOSSARY

adharma	moral demerit, opposite to or against moral duty
Advaita	Non-dualism, a branch of Vedānāta philosophy emphasizing the unity of the self with Brahman, the Ultimate Reality
akrasia	moral error
an-atman	no-self
anatma-vada	no-self theory; the Buddhist theory that all things are bereft of substance or permanent identical reality
Apabhramsa	corrupt or non-grammatical language
atman	Self, Spirit, that which manifests itself as the 'I'
atma-vada	the theory that the real is substance, permanent, eternal, and has the nature of its own
atmavidya	the knowledge of the Self
Baul	group of mystic mistrels from Bengal mainly consisting of Vaishnava Hindus and Sufi Muslims
bhakta	a devotee
bhakti	devotion, love
bhasha	language
Brahmavidya	the knowledge of the Brahman, who is the Ultimate Reality
Brahmodaya	dawn of Brahma
Chaturvarna	fourfold arrangement of socioeconomic categories which is based on caste consisting of Brahmins

	(priestly or scholarly caste), Kshatriya (martial or royal caste), Vaishyas (merchant caste) and Sudras (labour caste).
*darsana*s	philosophical systems
ditthi	view, belief, speculative opinion
Gurujadadiadugujada	We follow the footsteps of Gurajada
kanyasulkam	bride-money, contract to make payment to a father in consideration of his giving his daughter in marriage
khalnayak	anti-hero
Kural	a popular work on general ethics, political principles, and happy married life
Lokayata	materialist school of Indian philosophy
mahajana	great or distinguished men/many people, multitude of men
Mimāmsā	synthetic consideration, especially exegetical; a school of orthodox Indian philosophy
Nyāya	an orthodox school of Indian philosophy
paravidya	higher knowledge, knowledge of atman, of Brahman
prabandham	composition
prajña	wisdom, non-dual knowledge
Purva Mimāmsā	a school of Vedānta providing philosophical justification for the Vedic ritualism
Sahajiya	spontaneous understanding
Saiva Siddhanta	a school of Saivism, perfected Saivism
Saivism	a philosophical school that reveres Lord Shiva as the Supreme Being
sandhi	period between two ages
Sankhya	number; an orthodox school of Indian philosophy
sant	saint

Sarvajna	a Kannada poet, philosopher, and pragmatist
Sastri	a Brahmin, one who is well-versed in systems of knowledge
satyagrahi	revolutionary
shakapurushudu	man of the century
Siddha	one who has attained extraordinary powers as a result of yogic practice
Sruti	that which is heard, scripture, Veda, scriptural authority
swaraj	self-rule, independence
Syadvada	the doctrine that 'it can be', the doctrine of 'let it be so', a philosophical standpoint in Jainism
Vaishnava	the school of philosophy that reveres Lord Vishnu as the Supreme Being
Vaitalika	awakening bard
Vastusastra	science of architecture
Vedānta	end of Vedas, final conclusion of Vedic teaching
Vira Saiva	a particular Shaiva sect popular in Karnataka
yugakarta	man of the era

BIBLIOGRAPHY

Althusser, Louis. 1984. *Essays on Ideology*. London: Verso Books.

Ambedkar, B. R. 2010. *The Essential Writings of B. R. Ambedkar* (edited by Valerian Rodrigues), New Delhi: Oxford University Press.

Apparao, Gurajada. 2011. *Kanyasulkam*. Translated as *Girls for Sale* by Velcheru Narayana Rao. New Delhi: Penguin.

Aquinas, St. Thomas. 1920. *The Summa Theologica of St. Thomas Aquinas*. Translated by Fathers of the English Dominican Province, second and revised edition. Online Edition Copyright © 2003 by Kevin Knight.

Arudra. 1985. *Gurajada Gurupeetam*. Vijayawada: Navodaya Publishers.

Aurobindo, Sri. 1972. *Bande Mataram: Early Political Writings 1, Vol. 1.* Pondicherry: Sri Aurobindo Birth Centenary Library.

———. 1972. *The Harmony of Virtue: Early Cultural Writings, Vol. 3.* Pondicherry: Sri Aurobindo Birth Centenary Library.

———. 1972. *The Social and Political Thought, Vol. 15.* Pondicherry: Sri Aurobindo Birth Centenary Library.

———. 1972. *Supramental Manifestation and other Writings, Vol. 16.* Pondicherry: Sri Aurobindo Birth Centenary Library.

———. 1972. *The Synthesis of Yoga: Parts One and Two, Vol. 20.* Pondicherry: Sri Aurobindo Birth Centenary Library.

———. 1972. *Letters on Yoga: Part One and Two, Vol. 22.* Pondicherry: Sri Aurobindo Birth Centenary Library.

Barthes, Roland. 1997. 'The Death of the Author', in Stephen Heath (trans.), *Image-Music-Text*, pp. 142–8. New York: Hill and Wang.

Basham, A. L. 1971. 'Traditional Influences on the Thought of Mahatma Gandhi', in Ravindra Kumar (ed.), *Essays on Gandhian Politics: The Rowlatt Satyagraha of 1919*, pp. 17–42. Oxford: Clarendon Press.

Bhattacharyya, Kalidas. 1985. 'Some Problems Concerning Meaning', in B. K. Matilal and J. L. Shaw (eds), *Analytical Philosophy in Comparative Perspective*, pp. 173–87. Dordrecht: D. Reidel Publishing Company.

———. 1982. 'Traditional Indian Philosophy as Modern Indian Thinkers View It', in S.S. Rama Rao Pappu and R. Puligandla (eds), *Indian Philosophy: Past and Future*, pp. 171–224. New Delhi: Motilal Banarsidass Publisher.

———. 1975. *The Fundamentals of K. C. Bhattacharyya's Philosophy*. Kolkata: Saraswat Library.

Bhattacharyya, Krishna Chandra, 2011. *Implications of the Philosophy of Kant*, translated from Bengali by J. N. Mohanty and Tara Chatterjee, New Delhi: Indian Council of Philosophical Research, Oxford University Press.

———. 1983. 'The Concept of Philosophy', in Gopinath Bhattacharyya (ed.), *Studies in Philosophy*, pp. 462–79. New Delhi: Motilal Banarsidass Publisher.

———. 1984. 'Svaraj in Ideas', *Indian Philosophical Quarterly*, XI(4): 383–93 (reprinted).

Bhushan, Nalini and Jay Garfield (eds). 2011. *Indian Philosophy in English: From Renaissance to Independence*. New York: Oxford University Press.

Bilgrami, Akeel. 2006. 'Gandhi's Integrity: The Philosophy Behind the Politics', in A. Raghuramaraju (ed.), *Debating Gandhi: A Reader*, pp. 248–66. New Delhi: Oxford University Press.

Chatterjee, Partha. 1986. *Nationalist Thought and Colonial World: A Derivative Discourse?* New Delhi: Oxford University Press.

Coomaraswamy, Ananda K. 1996. *Hinduism and Buddhism*. New Delhi: Munshiram Manoharlal Publishers Pvt. Ltd.

———. 1981. *Essays in National Idealism*. New Delhi: Munshiram Manoharlal Pvt. Ltd.

Descartes, R. 1985. 'Discourse on Method', in John Cottingham, Robert Stoothoff, and Dugald Murdoch (trans.), *The Philosophical Writings of Descartes, Vol. I*, pp. 111–51. Cambridge: Cambridge University Press.

Devare, Aparna. 2011. *History and the Making of a Modern Hindu Self*. New Delhi: Routledge.

Foucault, Michel. 1994. 'What Is an Author?', in Robert Con Davis and Ronald Schliefer (eds), *Contemporary Literary Criticism: Literary and Cultural Studies*, pp. 341–53. New York: Longmans Publishing.

Foucault, Michel. 1984. 'What Is Enlightenment?', in Paul Rabinow (ed.), *The Foucault Reader*, pp. 32–50. New York: Pantheon Books.

Gandhi, M. K. 1976. *An Autobiography or The Story of My Experiments with Truth*. Ahmedabad: Navjivan Publishing House.

Gandhi, Ramchandra. 1983. 'Earthquake in Bihar: The Transfiguration of Karma', in Ramchandra Gandhi (ed.), *Language, Tradition & Modern Civilization*, pp. 125–53. Pune: Indian Philosophical Quarterly Publications.

Gellner, Ernest. 1983. *Nation and Nationalism*. Oxford: Basil Blackwell Publishing.

Guha, Ramachandra. 2008. 'The Challenge of Contemporary History', *Economic and Political Weekly*, 43(26–7): 192–200.

Guru, Gopal. 2002. 'How Egalitarian Are the Social Sciences in India', *Economic and Political Weekly*, XXVII(51): 5003–9.

Hume, Ernest. 2003. *The Thirteen Principal Upanishads*. Translated from Sanskrit by Ernest Hume, second edition. New Delhi: Oxford University Press.

Husserl, Edmond. 1970. *The Crisis of European Sciences and Transcendental Phenomenology: An Introduction to Phenomenology*. Trans. David Carr. Evanston: Northwestern University Press.

Joshi, Lal Mani. 1983. *Discerning the Buddha: A Study of Buddhism and the Brahmanical Hindu Attitude to It*. New Delhi: Munshiram Manoharlal Publishers Pvt. Ltd.

Kant, Immanuel. 1991. 'An Answer to the Question: What Is Enlightenment?', in Hans Reiss (ed.), H. B. Nisbet (trans.), *Kant's Political Writings*, pp. 54–60. Cambridge: Cambridge University Press.

Kaviraj, Sudipto. 2005. 'The Sudden Death of Sanskrit Knowledge', *Journal of Indian Philosophy*, 33(1): 119–42.

Krishna, Daya. 1996. *Indian Philosophy: A Counter Perspective*. New Delhi: Oxford University Press.

———. 1996a. *The Problematic and Conceptual Structure of Classical Indian Thought about Man, Society and Polity*. New Delhi: Oxford University Press.

Krishna, Daya, M. P. Rege, R.C. Dwivedi, and Mukund Lath. 1991. *Samvāda: A Dialogue between Two Philosophical Traditions*. New Delhi: Indian Council of Philosophical Research.

MacIntyre, Alasdair. 1985. *After Virtue*. London: Duckworth.

———. 2002. *A Short History of Ethics*. London: Routledge (Revised Edition).

Matilal, B. K. 2002. *The Collected Essays of Bimal Krishna Matilal: Ethics and Epic* (edited by Jonardan Ganeri), New Delhi: Oxford University Press.

McDermott, Robert A. and V. S. Naravane (eds). 2010. *The Spirit of Modern India*. Colorado: Lindisfarne Books (Reprint Edition).

Mehta, J. L. 1974. 'The Problem of Philosophical Reconception in the Thought of K. C. Bhattacharyya', *Philosophy East and West*, 24(1): 59–70.

Murti, T. R. V. 2010. *The Central Philosophy of Buddhism: A Study of Madhyamika System*. New Delhi: Munshiram Manoharlal Publishers Pvt. Ltd.

————. 1983. *Studies in Indian Thought: Collected Papers of T.R.V. Murti* (edited by Harold G. Coward). New Delhi: Motilal Banarsidass Publisher.

Murty, Satchidananda K. 1985. *Philosophy in India: Traditions, Teaching and Research*. New Delhi: Motilal Banarsidass Publishers.

Nagaraj, D. R. 1993. 'Self-purification v/s Self-respect: On the Roots of the Dalit Movement', in *The Flamming Feet: A Study of the Dalit Movement*, pp. 1–30. Bangalore: South Forum Press.

Naipaul, V. S. 2008. *A Writer's People: Ways of Looking and Feeling*. New York: Knopf Publishers.

Nandy, Ashis. 1994. *The Intimate Enemy: Loss and Recovery of Self under Colonialism*. New Delhi: Oxford University Press.

Nussbaum, Martha C. 1994. *The Therapy of Desire: Theory and Practice in Hellenistic Ethics*. Princeton: Princeton University Press.

Okin, S. M. 1989. 'Reason and Feeling in Thinking about Justice', *Ethics*, 99(2): 229–49.

Radhakrishnan, S. 2008. *Indian Philosophy, Vol. 1*. New Delhi: Oxford University Press.

Radhakrishnan, S. and J. H. Muirhead (eds). 1952. *Contemporary Indian Philosophy*. London: George Allen & Unwin.

Raghuramaraju, A. 2006. *Debates in Indian Philosophy: Classical, Colonial and Contemporary*. New Delhi: Oxford University Press.

————. 2011. *Modernity in Indian Social Theory*. New Delhi: Oxford University Press.

————. 2007. 'Krishna Chandra Bhattacharyya on the Unknowability of Self in Kant: Problematizing the Programme of Indian Remedies to Western Problems', in Bindu Puri and Heiko Sievers (eds), *Reason, Morality and Beauty: Essays on the Philosophy of Immanuel Kant*, pp. 134–51. New Delhi: Oxford University Press.

————. 2005. 'Rethinking the West', *Third Text*, 19(6): 595–8.

————. 2005a. 'Internal Project of Modernity and Post-Colonialism', *Economic and Political Weekly*, 40(39): 4214–18.

————. 2003. *Maidanam Lotulloki: Postmodern Pariseelana*. Vijayawada: Emesco Publishers.

Raman, N. S. S. 1989. 'T. R. V. Murti's interpretation of Buddhism', in S. Vijaya Kumar (ed.), *T. R. V. Murti and Indian Philosophical Tradition T. R. V. Murti Memorial Volume*, pp. 77–87. Varanasi: Department of Philosophy, Banaras Hindu University.

Ranade, R. D. 2012. 'The Problem of Ultimate Reality in Upanisads', in Nalini Bhushan and Jay Garfield (eds), *Indian Philosophy in English: From Renaissance to Independence*, pp. 245–67. New York: Oxford University Press.

Rao, Velcheru Narayana. 2011. 'A Play in Context: A Second Look at Apparao's Kanyasulkam', in *Kanyasulkam* (translated as *Girls for Sale* by Velcheru Narayana Rao). New Delhi: Penguin.

Raychaudhuri, Tapan. 1989. *Europe Reconsidered: Perception of the West in Nineteenth Century Bengal*. Delhi: Oxford University Press.

Renan, Ernest. 1939. *What Is a Nation?* New York: Oxford University Press.

Rorty, R. 1982. *Consequences of Pragmatism*. Minneapolis.

Rousseau, J. J. 1952. *The Social Contract and Discourse*. London: J. M. Dent & Sons Ltd.

Said, Edward. 1989. 'Representing the Colonized: Anthropology's Inter-locutors', *Critical Inquiry*, 15: 205–25.

————. 1986. 'Orientalism Reconsidered', in Francis Barker, Peter Hulms, Margaret Iverson, and Diana Loxley (eds), *Literature, Politics and Theory*, pp. 210–29. London: Methuen Publishing.

————. 1984. *The World, the Text and the Critic*. London: Faber and Faber.

————. 1979. *Orientalism*. New York: Vintage Books.

Samaddar, J. N. 1924. 'The Edicts of Asoka', *The Visva Bharati Quarterly*, 11(3): 239–50.

Sen, Amartya. 2005. *The Argumentative Indian: Writings on Indian Culture, History and Identity*. London: Penguin.

Sen, Amiya P. 1993. *Hindu Revivalism in Bengal 1872–1905: Some Essays in Interpretation*. Delhi: Oxford University Press.

Spengler, Oswald. 1991. *The Decline of the West*. Trans. C. F. Atkinson. Oxford: Oxford University Press.

Taylor, Charles. 1989. *Sources of the Self: The Making of Modern Identity*. Cambridge, Mass.

Vivekananda, Swami. 1994. *The Complete Works of Swami Vivekananda, Volumes I–VIII*. Kolkata: Advaita Ashram.

Walzer, M. 1983. *Spheres of Justice: A Defense of Pluralism and Equality*. Cambridge, Mass.

Williams, Raymond. 1986. 'Forms of English Fiction in 1848', in Francis Barker, Peter Hulms, Margaret Iverson, and Diana Loxley (eds), *Literature, Politics and Theory: Papers from the Essex Conference 1976–84*, pp. 1–16. London: Methuen Publishing.

INDEX

ABOUT THE AUTHOR

A. Raghuramaraju is Professor at the Department of Philosophy, University of Hyderabad. He has published widely in the areas of social and political philosophy; Indian philosophy; postmodernism and postcolonialism; bio-ethics; and science, technology, and society. He is also General Editor of *Porugununchi Teluguloki: Charcha Kosam, Vimarsha Kosam*, a series of Telugu translations of books on post-independence India. Apart from several published articles in journals and edited volumes, both in English and Telugu, his books include *Ramchandra Gandhi: The Man and His Philosophy* (ed., 2013), *Modernity in Indian Social Theory* (2011), *Enduring Colonialism: Classical Presences and Modern Absences in Indian Philosophy* (2009), *Debating Gandhi: A Reader* (ed., 2006), and *Debates in Indian Philosophy: Classical, Colonial and Contemporary* (2006). In 2007, *Debates in Indian Philosophy* was selected as a Choice Outstanding Academic Title by *CHOICE*, a premier magazine for reviews of academic books and e-media.